The
New Stock Index
Market

The
New Stock Index
Market

Strategies for Profit
in Stock Index Futures
and Options

Max G. Ansbacher

WALKER AND COMPANY ✺ NEW YORK

First published in the United States of America
in 1983 by the Walker Publishing Company, Inc.

Published simultaneously in Canada by John Wiley & Sons
Canada, Limited, Rexdale, Ontario.

Library of Congress Cataloging in Publication Data

Ansbacher, Max G.
   The new stock index market.

   Includes index.
   1.   Stock index futures.   I. Title.
HG6043.A57   1983   332.63'222   83–6525
ISBN 0–8027–0733–5

Library of Congress Cataloging Card Number: 83–6525

Printed in the United States of America

10 9 8 7 6 5 4 3 2 1

Contents

Preface   **1**

Chapter 1. Stock Indexes   **5**

2. What Are Stock Index Futures?   **16**

3. Basic Trading Strategies   **56**

4. Complex Trading Strategies   **95**

5. Options on Indexes   **101**

6. Selling Options   **128**

Appendixes

A. Specifications of Indexes   **160**

B. Glossary of Terms   **162**

C. Sources of More Information   **168**

D. The Eight Biggest Mistakes in Stock Index Trading   **171**

Index   **175**

Preface

Trading in stock indexes is not only the newest way of speculating in the stock market, but it is also both the most exciting and in many ways the easiest. Futures on the indexes were introduced in February 1982 and have already caught on with traders, speculators and hedgers in volume completely unexpected. Options on the indexes started trading on January 28, 1983 and promise to become even more popular than the futures. The reason for this tremendous popularity is that there are so many ways stock index trading can accomplish one's profit objectives.

This potential for profit was not possible for those who heretofore only traded stocks. For example, if you have believed on August 10, 1982 that after declining for months the stock market was ready to move up, and you were trading the stock-index futures, you could have bought a December contract for the Standard & Poor's 500 Index at a price of 102.60. This would require $6,000. Three months later, on November 10, you decide that the market has had a pretty good rally and so you sell the contract at its price then of 141.70. The result: a profit to you, after commissions, of $13,475, representing a profit on your $6,000 investment of 224%.

Try duplicating that by buying and selling stocks! And notice that there was nothing exotic here. No day trading, no fancy spreads, no trying to sell at the highs and buy at the lows, no increasing the size of your position as it went up. Just a simple process of purchasing a contract on August 10 and selling it three months later.

Although options on stock indexes were not being traded during this period, there is no doubt that profits this great and even much greater would have resulted if anyone had been able to buy the right call options on the Standard & Poor's 500 Index on August 10, 1982 and sold them three months later.

And this leads us to the other great advantage of trading in the

1

stock indexes. Not only is the potential for profit truly bountiful, as we have seen, but it is also very easy in one respect. For the very first time, it is possible to trade on the stock market without having to pick which specific stock or stocks you believe are going to perform the best. Just recall how many times in the past you had a conviction that the stock market was going to move either down or up, and you then selected a stock or stocks which you believed would lead the move. And then how many times were you absolutely right in your belief about which way the stock market would move, only to find to your dismay that the particular stocks you selected didn't move with the market! Now the problem of not picking the right stocks is over. You can literally play "the market" as a whole. If you believe the market is going up, you can go long a futures contract, or buy an option on a stock index. If you believe it is going to go down, you short an index future, or buy a put on one of the indexes. In either event, if you are just right on the direction of the market, you will make money. And with the built-in leverage of both the futures and the options on the indexes, you can make a great deal of money indeed.

Picking the market rather than individual stocks is so much more satisfying in other respects too. At last there are no more surprises in store, like suddenly reading in your morning newspaper that the one company whose stock you really loaded up on is reporting a totally unexpected loss this quarter because of fraud in one of its divisions, or sales of its hot new product are down, or it was just sued by its best customer, or its products suddenly turn out to have been fatal or carcinogenic. Why go on? You know the problem. With the indexes you can rise above all these coronary causers.

Furthermore, trading the indexes is much less time-consuming because you don't have to get bogged down in the details of scores of different companies. If you are a serious student of the stock market, you know what a tremendous amount of time must be spent poring over corporate annual reports, quarterly reports, brokerage house reports and recommendations, newspaper and magazine accounts of industries and companies, market letter advice and so forth. Following each industry and each company in the industry is an eye-popping task. What are the sales forecasts? How is the industry doing this year? What is the forecast for next year? Will they have the high-profit products? How good is their management compared to that of the competition? What is the effect of imports on the market? What is their ratio of debt to equity? What's their five-year growth rate been? What are their long-term prospects? How will the changes in the economy affect them? It goes on forever.

Now, with the new stock indexes you can leave this mass of details behind you. This time you just look at the overall picture, using information readily available in your daily newspaper. How the economy is doing, and where it is likely to be in the future are the main questions, along with what is happening to interest rates and other macroeconomic factors. So instead of trying to keep up with what the president of a candy company thinks profits on bubble gum will be next year, you can pay more attention to what the chairman of the Federal Reserve Board thinks about the money supply.

Maybe your view of the economy convinces you that certain groups of stocks might do very well, or that they might do very poorly. In this case the general indexes won't help you very much, but trading on one of the new subindexes could be the perfect vehicle for you. There are (or soon will be) indexes on groups of companies involved in finances, oil, computers, aerospace/air transport, drugs, hospital management and supplies, electronic instrumentation, media/entertainment, metals and oil services. The advantages of using these indexes instead of individual stocks are the leverage they afford and the elimination of the need to pick individual companies.

The stock-index futures now offer the leverage of commodities to the stock market. For those who have been in the stock market but have never traded commodities before, the technique involved may be confusing. One of the major purposes of this book is to explain how futures contracts work in general, how they work specifically with respect to stock indexes, and what you can do about avoiding the terrible fate of being locked in and losing more than you ever planned to place at risk in the first place.

For those who want a precise limit on their exposure, the new options on stock indexes offer an exciting and challenging medium. The options can be even more challenging than the futures because of the many different strike prices available, and this book explains in detail just which strike prices offer the biggest advantages for trading both puts and calls. Further, there are discussions on which expiration period to select, as well as chapters on selling puts and calls.

All this is not to say that stock indexes are the Garden of Financial

Eden. Both the futures and the options on stock indexes are risky and should be used only by people who want to speculate with money they can afford to lose. Neither options nor futures on the indexes are investments by themselves, although in conjunction with other financial assets they may make up a small but very appropriate part of an investment portfolio. Lest anyone think it is easy to make money on the indexes, just remember that futures are a zero-sum activity, which means that unlike the stock market, for every dollar someone makes, a dollar must be lost by someone else. The whole purpose of this book is to try to shift the odds so they will be as favorable as possible for you to be the one making the money.

In summary, there is no question that these new futures and options on stock indexes offer leverage and profit opportunities never before available to stock traders. The opportunity is there for those who have the financial resources and suitable emotional temperament. But the risks are equally as real, and before you learn the hard way by losing real dollars, it behooves you to know about the traps before you risk your dollars. Anyone not familiar with these two new markets will make mistakes. You can learn about the risks either by reading this book and trading on paper for a time, or by opening an account and learning from actual trial and error. Either way you will learn, but I believe quite strongly that if you learn from actual trading, you will pay far more for the learning experience than you will for this book.

CHAPTER 1
Stock Indexes

Trading stock-index futures and options is the newest way to speculate on Wall Street, but the underlying stock indexes have been around for many years. It's just that up until now there has been no way to trade them directly. The fact that the indexes themselves are familiar to millions of investors helps in understanding how to trade them. As an example of their familiarity, probably everyone in the United States today over four years of age has heard the Dow Jones Industrial Average announced on the evening network television news. The Dow Jones is certainly the best known of all the indexes, but the others we are going to discuss are very similar to it.

Actually, there is no trading in the Dow Jones index at the time of this writing because the owner of that average, Dow Jones & Co., Inc., does not want its distinguished name used as a vehicle for speculation. When the Commodity Exchange, Inc., in New York tried to trade futures on an index identical to the Dow Jones average, Dow Jones & Co. sued them in court and was able to prevent trading from ever starting. Nevertheless, the general indexes which are traded have marked similarities to the Dow Jones average.

The ones we are going to describe are the New York Stock Exchange Index, with futures traded on the New York Futures Exchange; the Standard & Poor's 500 Index, with futures traded on the Index and Option Market Division of the Chicago Mercantile Exchange; the Value Line Composite Average, with futures traded on the Kansas City Board of Trade; the CBOE–100, which has options traded on the Chicago Board Options Exchange; the Major Market Index with options traded on the American Stock Exchange and sub-indexes on various groups of stocks, such as financial or computer stocks.

What all of these indexes have in common is that they collect the prices of a large number of stocks and average them into one number, which then reflects the prices of all those stocks. The need for such an average arose years ago, when one investor would ask another how the stock market was doing. Without an index, the only answer would be that it was up a lot, or down a little, but it would be impossible to give a quantitative answer to the question. Quoting the prices of a number of individual stocks would give a sampling of how the market was doing but would be time-consuming and not necessarily indicative of the market as a whole. Since necessity is the mother of invention, the idea of averaging stocks together was born, and then one could sum up the performance of the entire stock market with one number. Very neat. Thus the term "index" is simply a synonym for an average.

We all learned in fourth grade how an average works. You simply add up the numbers you want to average, in this case the prices of the various stocks, and then divide by the total number of stocks. It's so simple that one wonders why there are so many different indexes. Shouldn't there be just one? Is one better than the others? Not too surprisingly, each futures or options exchange sincerely believes that *its* index is superior to the others in many ways. Since we intend to make money by trading them, let's get into the details of the various indexes to see the advantages and disadvantages of each one.

DOW JONES INDUSTRIAL AVERAGE

The most elementary of all is the Dow Jones Industrial Average, which I will refer to as the Dow Jones or as the DJIA. To compile this average, the stock prices of thirty large industrial companies are added up, then that total is divided by 30. This was the original method, but because there have been so many stock splits and stock dividends, the result must now be adjusted to take these changes into consideration. Nevertheless, the basic process is averaging just as you learned back in fourth grade.

One thing to be said in its favor is its simplicity. But why do they use only thirty stocks? The New York Stock Exchange lists over fifteen hundred stocks, the American Stock Exchange lists about two thousand and there are thousands more traded over the counter. Can a mere thirty stocks be truly representative of this large group? The answer is not only "no," but further, that the Dow Jones was not intended to be a real stock market index. It is deliberately aimed as an index only of large, well-established industrial companies. These stocks do not necessarily move with the rest of the market. They may not move with small oil companies, or with new high-technology companies, or with financial companies such as banks and insurance companies. Therefore, on the basis of its stock input, the Dow Jones is a poor index upon which to judge the stock market as a whole. Or to be practical, if you thought that the stock market as a whole were going to go up, that wouldn't necessarily mean that the Dow Jones would go up.

Second, let's look at the mathematics of calculating this average. Because the result is obtained by adding up all the prices and dividing, this means that a change of $1 in a stock has the same effect no matter which stock changes by that much. For example, let's say that a $20 stock goes up by $1, and a $200 stock goes up by $1. The result to the Dow Jones average will be identical, and yet one stock has gone up by 5% and the other by only ½%. Is this accurate? Or let's suppose that they both go up by 5%. The $20 stock goes up by $1, and the $200 stock goes up by $10. So the change in the $200 stock has ten times the impact upon the Dow Jones as the $20 stock, yet they both went up by the same percentage! This is the problem with the arithmetical method used in computing the Dow Jones Industrial Average.

A third problem arises from the fact that all stocks are treated equally. Thus if stock A goes up by $0.50 it will have the same impact upon the average as if stock B goes up by $0.50. And yet stock A may have relatively few shares of stock, whereas company B is the biggest industrial company in the world, whose shares are included in virtually every portfolio in America. Therefore a change in the price of stock B is many times more important than that of stock A, yet they are treated identically in the Dow Jones Industrial Average. So if you want an index which is telling you what the effect of stock prices is on the value of stock ownership, the Dow Jones may be quite misleading.

STANDARD & POOR'S 500 INDEX

Standard & Poor's 500 Index, known as the S&P 500, has made an effort to overcome some of the disadvantages of the Dow Jones. In the first place, instead of just thirty stocks, it is comprised of five hundred stocks. Compiled by Standard & Poor's Corporation, which also publishes various stock market guides and gives bond ratings, it began as the S&P 200 in 1917 and was expanded to embrace five hundred stocks in 1957. And unlike the Dow Jones, which is made up of industrial stocks only, the S&P 500 includes four hundred industrial companies plus forty public utilities, twenty transportation companies and forty financial companies. They are mainly traded on the New York Stock Exchange, but some are on the American Stock Exchange, and some are over the counter. These stocks represent approximately 80% of the value of all issues traded on the New York Stock Exchange.

The other major difference between the S&P 500 and the Dow Jones is that the S&P 500 recognizes the fact that some stocks are more important than others, because they represent far bigger companies. Before the average is taken, the price of each stock is multiplied by the number of shares outstanding. Therefore, if a stock has ten thousand shares outstanding, and it goes up by $1, it will be weighted ten times as heavily as a stock which has only a thousand shares outstanding. This means that the S&P 500 gives a much better picture of what actual effect price changes have on the values of people's stock holdings and therefore makes it a superior index for most purposes.

It is for these reasons that the S&P 500 has become the standard by which most professional money managers measure their progress. In fact, it has even been recognized by the United States government, which uses the S&P 500 as the stock market component of its leading indicators index, which uses the movement of the stock market as one of its indications of the future course of the economy.

The method of arriving at the final price is similar to the Dow Jones—that is, the prices multiplied by the number of shares are added up and then divided by 500. This means that an increase of equal percentage is not treated equally for stocks of different prices; for example, as we mentioned in our discussion of the DJIA, a 2% increase in a $200 stock will get ten times as much weight as a 2% increase in a $20 stock. Thus the percentage increase in the S&P 500 may not be precise. The S&P 500 futures are traded on the Index and Option Market Division of Chicago Mercantile Exchange.

NEW YORK STOCK EXCHANGE INDEX
The New York Stock Exchange (NYSE) Index is very similar to the S&P 500 Index. The major difference is that instead of using five hundred selected stocks, the NYSE Index uses every stock listed on the New York Stock Exchange, currently over 1,520 stocks. Every other aspect of computing the index is the same—that is, it is a

mathematical average which is weighted according to the number of shares outstanding. Therefore, to compute the NYSE Index one first multiplies the price of each share by the number of shares outstanding. These figures are all added up and divided by the total number of stocks, then divided by the number of shares outstanding. Thus it is a weighted index, so that a move in a widely held stock such as IBM will have far more weight than that of a small company. It is computed every minute during the trading day, as is the S&P 500.

As with all the indexes, the resulting number must then be multiplied by a factor to reflect all the changes which have come about since its inception due to stock splits, stock dividends, and reorganizations.

The index was introduced at the end of 1965 and arbitrarily set at 50. It is interesting to note that simply because the NYSE started out with the number 50 in 1965, the current NYSE Index is about half the figure for the S&P 500 and the Value Line Composite Average.

THE VALUE LINE COMPOSITE AVERAGE

The Value Line Composite Average (VLCA) is the most sophisticated of all the indexes. First, it is based upon a selection of approximately seventeen hundred different stocks, 90% of which are traded on the New York Stock Exchange, and the rest of which are traded on the American Stock Exchange or over the counter. These stocks are the ones followed by the Value Line Investment Survey, to which many investors subscribe. In fact, the Value Line Composite Average is published by the Arnold Bernhard Co. of New York City, which publishes the Survey, and the futures are traded on the Kansas City Board of Trade under license from the Arnold Bernhard Co. The stocks which make up the VLCA account for 96% of all dollar trading volume in U.S. equity markets.

The big difference between the VLCA and the NYSE and S&P 500 indexes is that it is not weighted by the importance of a stock as indicated by the number of shares outstanding. This means that a change in a little over-the-counter stock is given the same importance as a change in IBM or GM. In this respect it is like the Dow Jones. But, of course, the Dow Jones Industrial Average is made up of only thirty stocks, and they are all quite widely held. The VLCA comprises so many stocks that most of them are not widely held. The result is that the VLCA can differ markedly from the other two indexes because the small stocks have a much greater relative importance to the VLCA than they do in the others. The small stocks also have a much greater importance in the VLCA than they would in the typical portfolio. Whether you believe that this makes this a good or a poor index depends upon your purpose in wanting to use the index, but it is an important distinction which must be kept in mind. Just remember that the VLCA is overrepresented by the movement of the many small-capitalization companies.

So far, all the indexes we studied were prepared by simple mathematical averaging. The VLCA is prepared in a more sophisticated manner. While the actual manner of computing it is too technical to describe, the net result is that the percentage change in the price of each stock is averaged. Therefore, in this index a percentage change of 1% in a $20 stock is given equal importance with a 1% change in a $200 stock. This would appear to be a more desirable result, but note the outcome: The price changes in low-priced stocks are given relatively more weight than in the other indexes. Thus if the prices of low-priced, small-company stocks are rising faster than others, the VLCA will go up faster than other averages.

THE CBOE-100 INDEX

This index is newer and less well known than the previously mentioned stock indexes. Although it was begun in January 1976 by the Chicago Board Options Exchange, its existence was virtually a secret until 1982, when the exchange began to publicize it prior to instituting trading on it. Unlike the indexes previously described, no futures are traded with the CBOE Index, just options.

The CBOE-100 comprises the prices of a hundred stocks which have options traded on the Chicago Board Options Exchange. It is weighted according to the number of shares outstanding, like the S&P 500 and the NYSE indexes. Because it is restricted to a hundred stocks which have listed options, it therefore tends to give large weight to the movement of the large-capitalization stocks. Included in the hundred stocks are such blue chips as IBM, AT&T, General Motors, General Electric, Eastman Kodak and Exxon.

The CBOE-100 has a high degree of correlation to the S&P 500 and the NYSE indexes. Analysis of daily price movements of the CBOE-100 from January 1976 through June 1982 shows a .98 correlation out of a possible 1.00.

THE MAJOR MARKET INDEX

The newest of the indexes is the Major Market Index, which was introduced by the American Stock Exchange on April 22, 1983. Like the CBOE–100 Index, there are no futures traded on the Major Market Index, only options.

The Major Market Index is also the simplest. It is comprised of the prices of just twenty stocks, all of which are major blue chips, such as American Express, Coca-Cola, Dow Chemical, Kodak, Exxon, General Electric, General Motors, etc. This index is not weighted by the number of shares outstanding. In fact, when the index originated, to get the actual number of the index, one simply added up the prices of all the shares and divided by 10. As splits, stock dividends and other changes in stocks occur, this simplicity will have to give way to a more complicated formula.

Since this index is comprised of only the bluest of the blue chips, and is not weighted by capitalization, it can be expected to have a very high corollary with the Dow Jones Industrial Average, which is computed in exactly the same manner on thirty blue chip stocks.

THE SUBINDEXES

The first subindex, also known as a group index, was the Financial Index of the New York Futures Exchange (NYFE), which began trading on November 12, 1982. It consists of the average of the prices of 212 financial services company shares listed on the New York Stock Exchange. The companies include banks, insurance companies and brokerage firms. The NYFE also planned to offer subindexes on a utilities group, a transportation group and an industrial group.

The Chicago Board Options Exchange planned to offer options on at least six group indexes. These are: the Aerospace Group, comprised of Boeing, Raytheon, General Dynamics, Rockwell International and United Technologies; the Air Transport Group, comprised of Delta Air Lines, Federal Express, Northwest Air, UAL and Southwest Air; the Computer Group, composed of Control Data, Honeywell, IBM, Sperry and NCR; the Drug Group, consisting of Bristol-Myers, Merck, Squibb, Syntex and Upjohn; the Paper and Forest Products Group, made up of Boise Cascade, Champion International, International Paper, Weyerhaeuser and Owens-Illinois; and the Petroleum Group, composed of Atlantic Richfield, Mobil, Superior Oil, Exxon and Standard Oil (Indiana).

The trading unit of the CBOE group indexes is a hundred shares of each of the group members, for a total of five hundred shares per group.

The American Stock Exchange planned subindexes on eleven industry groups. Most of the stocks making up the groups trade on the New York Stock Exchange. The subindexes are: Electronic Instrumentation and Components, made up of thirty-four stocks; Aerospace/Air Transport, eleven stocks; Drugs, fourteen stocks; Financial Services, thirty stocks; Hospital Management and Supplies, fourteen stocks; Informational Technology, twenty-nine stocks; Media/Entertainment, twenty-seven stocks; Merchandising, forty-two stocks; Metals, twenty-eight stocks; Oil and Gas, twenty stocks; and Oil Services, eighteen stocks.

HOW THE INDEXES MOVE IN RELATION TO EACH OTHER

You may think that this has been a very interesting discussion on mathematics, but you didn't buy this book to become a learned mathematician, you bought it to learn how to make money. So what difference does it make, in trying to make money, which index you use? It can make a lot of difference, and it is important that you know which index will best suit your objectives. Just consider the following figures:

Over the ten-year period 1970 to 1980, the Dow Jones Industrial Average went up 15%, the Value Line Composite Average went up 39%, the S&P 500 went up 47% and the NYSE Index went up 56%. Although we are not going to use these indexes for long-term investing, just think what a difference it would make to you if you were long (that is, had bought) any of these averages for that period. And the difference during short periods of time can be significant also.

For example, when you are buying a futures contract, one of the things you want to know is how far the index is likely to move on a particular day. How far can it move in your favor to make money for you? How much is it likely to move against you so you will lose money? As you might expect, the NYSE and the S&P 500 are quite similar in their movements, since both are weighted arithmetic averages of a large number of stocks. The VLCA is quite different, since it is unweighted and therefore gives proportionally more weight to a lot of smaller stocks, which are generally more volatile than the blue chips.

Here are some statistics on just how the indexes move in an average day. From observations during the period January 1, 1975 to March 11, 1982, it has been calculated that the mean (average) daily move was $0.29 for the NYSE, $0.53 for the S&P 500 and $0.45 for the VLCA. Since these are absolute numbers, keep in mind that the price of the NYSE Index is about half that of the other two. To keep them in proportion, double the movement in the NYSE Index. So they are really not that different. A completely different story emerges, however, if we look at the most extreme moves made. During the same period, if we examine the daily move made on the 1% of all days when they made their greatest moves, we find that the NYSE moved $1.48, the S&P 500 moved $2.69 and the VLCA moved $4.28. If we double the change in the NYSE to make it comparable, we have $2.96, which, as we expected, is quite close to that of the S&P 500. But look at the VLCA. That move is a full 60% more than the others. And if we look at the really extreme moves, the differences become even greater. Taking the ½% of the days when the greatest moves occurred—in other words just looking at the biggest move in two hundred days—we find that the NYSE was $1.80 (which doubled is $3.60), the S&P 500 was $3.17 and the VLCA was $7.51. Again, the NYSE and the S&P 500 are quite close to one another, but the VLCA is over twice as great.

The moral is clear. If you want an index which can really spurt up or down, your choice is the VLCA. But if you want a steadier index, you would pick either the S&P 500 or the NYSE.

One major difference between the CBOE-100 and the Major Market Index, and the other indexes is that to translate a move of a point of these indexes into actual dollars and cents to the speculator, a factor of $100 is used, rather than the $500 used for the others. Thus a move up of 2 points on the CBOE-100 is a move of $200, whereas a move up of 2 points on the other indexes is equal to $1,000.

Another point is that if you believe the big blue chips are going to lead a rally on Wall Street, then obviously you would choose the NYSE or the S&P, and you would probably go for the S&P, since that excludes all but the five hundred biggest stocks. On the other hand, once a bull market has gotten under way and the big blue-chip stocks have reached a fully priced level, it may be time for the second-or third-tier stocks to begin their moves up. If those were your thoughts, you would go long the VLCA.

Suppose that the market has been quite high, and you believe it will begin to decline and want to short one of the indexes. Quite frequently the lesser-quality stocks begin to lose first. In that case you would short the VLCA. This is exactly what happened in the great bear market of 1973–74. The VLCA turned down fully eight to ten months before the S&P 500 and the NYSE began to reflect the bear-market decline. This also occurred in the really great crash of 1929. In 1929 the equal weighted index, which is what the VLCA is, reached its peak six months before the peak of the other two, indicating that the small stocks, which are so heavily represented in the VLCA, started to turn down before the larger ones. Clearly, this is of great value if you believe that the market has reached a high and is about to turn down. Your strategy would be to go short the VLCA. But if you believe that a bull market is going to continue, avoid the VLCA but stay long the NYSE or S&P 500, all the while keeping a sharp eye out for the action of the VLCA.

Thus, while all the indexes generally move in the same direction at the same time, the VLCA tends to be more volatile and may indicate some major moves before the other indexes. In fact, one book, *The Stock Market: Theories and Evidence* by James A. Lorie and Mary T. Hamilton (Homewood, Ill.: Richard D. Irwin, 1973) concluded that not only is an equal weighted index like the VLCA more appropriate for indicating movements in the prices of typical stocks, but also that it is better at indicating the expected change in prices of stocks.

CONCLUSIONS

To summarize this chapter, the indexes will move together most of the time, and usually by similar percentages. While the S&P 500, the NYSE, the Major Market Index and the CBOE-100 are quite similar in their action, the method of computing the NYSE results in its final index number being about half the value of the others. In this chapter we have discussed changes in terms of percent. In the world of Wall Street one usually thinks of changes in these terms and in how many points (dollars) or cents the indexes have moved. Since the NYSE is about half the price of the S&P 500, a similar percentage change in the stock market will change the NYSE by only half as much as the S&P 500.

Two main differences stand out. The NYSE, S&P 500, the Major Market Index and CBOE-100 are very similar in their composition; therefore your decision on which of these to use will be determined by factors of the futures contract, such as margin and commissions, rather than anything to do with the underlying index. Vis-à-vis the VLCA, the two differences are: (1) on those unusual days when there are big moves in the market, expect the VLCA to move much farther than the other two. This is because when the market moves down, the second- and third-tier stocks tend to move down faster than the blue chips; and when the market takes a really big move up, often the staid old blue chips don't leap up like the hot stocks of the day. This means that if you really have faith in your point of view, you would go into the VLCA, but if you are cautious and realize that you could be on the wrong side and are therefore worried about your exposure if the market makes a major move against you, then you would tend to avoid the VLCA. (2) At some major changes in the market, the VLCA might move before the other two indexes. If you expect that move, go with the VLCA, but if you are betting on a continuation of the present trend, then avoid it. As a gross oversimplification, if you want a wild and exciting ride, saddle up a VLCA contract and watch out. If you want a somewhat more even ride, hitch your wagon to the S&P 500, NYSE, the Major Market Index or CBOE-100.

CHAPTER 2
What Are Stock Index Futures?

Now that we have learned about the stock-market indexes, we can find out about one of the methods by which we trade these indexes. And that is by going either long or short a future on the index. While futures trading has a long and distinguished history in the commodities market, it really isn't necessary to go into that to understand how futures work with respect to stock indexes. The simplest explanation of how a future works is to imagine that you are buying the index today. If you believe that the index will move up, you buy it, which in financial language is to go long the future. If you figure that the index is going to go down, you would sell it, expressed as going short, and in commodities it is just as easy to go short as it is to go long.

When you buy a stock, you own it until you sell it. But in the world of commodities, you buy or sell something for a specific period. These periods vary, and you will have your choice as to how long you wish to be either long or short your contract. The contracts expire every three months—specifically, in March, June, September and December. For the VLCA and the S&P 500 you can choose any expiration you want for the next four expiration periods, and for the NYSE there is a choice of the next six expirations. For various reasons which we will discuss later, the different months will be selling at different prices.

TRADING BASICS
Let's say that you are bullish on the stock market and are considering going long a contract. You decide that you will pick one of the indexes, which is listed at 130. You pick a future of that index with an expiration month which is currently trading at 133. You tell your broker to buy it for you, which he does at that price. What does this

mean? In effect you have bought the contract for a price of 133 just as if you had bought a stock for $133.

But here instead of buying a stock, you have in effect bought a number representing a collection of stocks called an index. The actual value of the futures you bought is 133 multiplied by $500. The $500 is simply an arbitrary figure used to determine the dollar value of the indexes. This means you have actually purchased a number representing a collection of stocks priced at 500 times 133, or $66,500.

Let us assume that you bought a December contract. One of the major differences between going long a stock-index-future contract and buying some shares of stock is that your investment in the index will come to an end at the expiration date in December. On that date, if you have not sold it before then, you will automatically be treated as if you sold it on the expiration date for the exact closing price of the index.

Let's look at our example. You bought the December contract for 133. The fact that the index was 130 when you went long your contract is irrelevant for our purposes here. Now you have your contract, and time passes by, and it is now the expiration date in December for your contract. Let us assume that the index has moved up to 135. That will be the closing (settlement) price on the expiration date. If you do nothing, you will be treated as if you sold your contract for 135 on the expiration date. Every point in a stock-index-futures contract is worth $500. Since you bought the contract for 133 and in effect sold it for 135, you have a profit of 2 points. Two times $500 is $1,000, and you will be credited with $1,000 in your account.

If the contract had settled at 130 on the expiration date, you would be treated as if you had sold it for that price, for a loss of three points, and your account would be charged that times $500, or $1,500. It is as simple as that.

Actually, the profit or loss in commodities accounts is calculated every day. This means that you can make or lose money from the very minute you trade. In our example you went long a December contract for 133. Let us assume that later in the day the market went up, and your December contract closed at 134. You would now be ahead by $500, and this would be your actual unrealized profit on the trade. That money would be credited to your account, and the next day you could take it out of the account and spend it. This is another big difference between commodities futures and buying stock. If you bought a share of stock for $133 and the next day it went up to $134, you might be able to tell yourself that you had a paper profit of $1, but you couldn't ask your brokerage firm to send it to you. They would say that if you decide to sell the stock, then they will be happy to send you the entire price, but in the meantime there is no way you can get that money (unless you borrow it against a margin account), and hence it is merely a paper profit.

The fact that you can get your profit out right away on a stock-index future is due to the fact that commodity accounts are "marked to the market" after the close of each day. This means that the commodity margin departments figure what your profit or loss would have been if you had closed out your account at the settlement price. While this is very nice if you are making money, it also means that when you lose money you have to bring in more money to your account immediately.

MARGIN FOR FUTURES

This brings us to one final difference between stock-index futures and buying a stock. If you buy a stock for $133, you would typically send in a check for that amount. If you wanted to buy it on margin, you would send in a check for half that amount, but that was because you decided you wanted to borrow half the amount from your brokerage firm and pay the firm their current interest rate on the amount of the loan. In commodities there is no such thing as paying the full price. Instead you pay only the amount of the required margin, and there is no interest charge on the balance. Another major difference is that the amount of the margin required has nothing to do with the price of the contract. It is determined in advance by the futures exchange and your brokerage firm. The current margin amounts for the stock indexes are $3,500 for the NYSE; $6,000 for the S&P 500; and $6,500 for the VLCA. The margin requirement is the same whether you want to buy (go long) a contract, or to sell (go short) a contract. As this book is written that is more or less 10% of the value of each contract.

Let's follow through with our example to see how this works. You bought one December contract at $133. Immediately your account will require the initial margin, which, if it is in the S&P 500, is $6,000. So to get started in trading stock-index futures, all you have to do is open a commodity account with a brokerage firm and deposit the initial margin, here $6,000. You buy your December contract for

$133. Let's assume that it closes that day at 133. Your account shows that you are long one December contract and that you have a credit in your account of $6,000, which is applied to the initial margin requirement. The next day the price of your December contract goes up to $134. At the end of business that day your account shows that you have a 1-point gain, which is multiplied by $500 to give you a credit of $500, plus the $6,000 you sent in. Of this amount, $500 will be excess, and you can take that out of the account if you want to.

Let's suppose that the next day you are not so fortunate and your December contract falls by two points. This means that at the end of the day your account will be reduced by two points multiplied by $500, or $1,000. Subtracting $1,000 from your previous credit of $6,500 gives you a balance of $5,500. Even though this is below your initial maintenance, you do not have to send in any more money until your balance falls by more than 25% of your original margin requirement, which in this case would be under $4,500.

And so it goes for as long as you own that December contract. When you decide to sell it, your account is marked to the market at the selling price, and your entire balance becomes free for you to withdraw. If you hold onto the contract until it expires, on the final day the account is marked to the market at the closing price of the index itself. And just as if you had sold the contract, it disappears from your account and you can withdraw your entire balance.

Thus there is nothing complicated about entering the stock-index futures game. It is just like buying stock, with these three basic differences: (1) You are buying or shorting something which has a limited time span and ceases to exist at the expiration of the designated month. (2) All trades are made on margin, and the amount is very small (about 10%), with no interest charge on what you don't pay. (3) The account is treated as if you realized your gains and losses at the end of every day. This "marking to the market" means you can take out your profits from the first day, but you also have to put in money if your position moves against you by more than 25% of the initial margin.

The above description, brief as it is, really tells what you need to know to understand trading stock-index futures. But this is a simplification of what happens. Any commodities experts reading this book must have shuddered at some of my comparisons to buying stock, because the traditional approach to commodities is so different. And since stock-index futures are now treated as a commodity, we really should be familiar with the theory of commodities and the technical aspects of commodities to know what is going on in stock futures.

TRADITIONAL COMMODITIES TRADING

Commodities trading began well over a century ago, and while we may think of commodities traders as speculators who take chances to get rich quick, all the commodities exchanges publish booklets explaining that the role of commodities futures is really to help the farmer get a decent price for his harvest, help the baker buy flour at a reasonably low cost and let the miller make a living in between them, thus making the United States of America a much better place in which you and I can live. Luckily we can leave the philosophizing to someone else and look at what actually happens. Typically when farm crops like wheat were being bought and sold before commodity futures, there was a dramatic seasonal difference in the price. As the harvest was being brought in, the farmers were anxious to sell every bushel because they needed the money to pay off their debts. But the buyers of wheat had probably already met the needs of their customers for the next month or so and therefore didn't want to tie up their capital by buying more. So the price of wheat dropped and farmers got a much lower price. But then as the winter came and no supplies of wheat were coming to market, the price of wheat would rise. This meant that the baker was paying much more for his purchases. Finally, in early spring before the new harvest came to market, there would be no wheat for sale, most of the existing supplies would have been used up and the price would start going sky high. But this didn't help the farmers, because at that time they didn't have any for sale.

Then when the harvest started to come in, the cycle would repeat itself as the new supply would be so great that the price would plunge. The result in this simplified example was that the farmer was always receiving a low price for his wheat, and the users of the wheat were often paying a higher price than they should have. It seemed that everyone lost. Could anything be done to remedy this deplorable situation?

Shazam! Enter our hero, the commodities future market! Someone looked at this situation and said, "This is ridiculous. The baker knows in the summer that he will be needing wheat early next spring, if only there were some way that he could lock in a price for next spring's delivery of wheat at something like this winter's prices. And the farmer desperately needs money in the winter and knows that he is going to have wheat for sale in a few months. If only there were some way that he could sell wheat in the winter for delivery in the summer." And so, the makings were there for the first commodities future exchange.

Farmers, bakers and middlemen got together and began to buy and sell wheat today with a price fixed today, for delivery at some future time. For example, if it were the winter, the farmer would be interested in selling wheat today at a specific price which he would promise to deliver in June or July. The purchaser of the June wheat contract didn't have to pay for the wheat until it was delivered in June, but to ensure that he lived up to his bargain, he did have to make a small payment now, which was called a "good-faith deposit." This was not margin in the sense of buying a share of stock on margin, because the purchaser was not buying any wheat today. He was only promising to purchase that wheat in June, and he would pay for it then. The entire purpose of this exercise was to establish now a fixed price for a transaction which was going to take place in June.

But how did this help the farmer? Although he didn't receive much money from his sale of the future, he was now guaranteed a certain price for his wheat. And even if the harvest was the biggest in the history of the West and the country were plunged into a major depression, so that the price of wheat plunged to all-time lows when the harvest finally arrived, that wouldn't make any difference to this farmer. Because, thanks to the futures exchange, he had gotten, in the winter, a guaranteed price for his harvest time delivery. Now that he had a guaranteed price for his crop, in a separate transaction he could take that guarantee to his local banker and get a loan to pay for his expenses in raising the crop.

Middlemen also benefited, because they could now lock in a fixed price for filling their storage silos in the summer. Then they would sell a contract due next winter to the baker, so that the middleman would have his costs and selling price all settled in advance. And the baker was able to ensure that he would have all the wheat he needed next winter at a reasonable price.

This is how the traditional commodities futures contract works, and the brand-new stock-index futures have been tailored to fit into this mold. Of course, there is all the difference in the world between a baker wanting to get delivery of wheat next winter and a speculator who would like to make money because he thinks the stock market is going to go up or down. But we will come to that.

SPECIAL ASPECTS OF COMMODITY FUTURES

There are a number of points worth noting in our wheat futures example. First, no wheat actually changes hands when the futures contracts are executed. Rather, this is a contract made now for future performance. The delivery date of the wheat is approximately the expiration date of the contract. Second, very little money changes hands. Each party to the contract places a deposit with the exchange, or actually with his broker, to ensure that he will fulfill his end of the bargain. But since there is no purchase and sale made now, there is no need for a large amount of money to change hands now. That will happen when the wheat is delivered. Third, the price of the wheat is fixed at the present time, and the price fixed in the contract is probably not the price of wheat in the current market.

For example, if the contracts are made in the spring a few months before the current crop, the price of wheat might be $4 a bushel then. But when the farmer sells a contract for later delivery, both he and the buyer of that contract are aware that there will be a lot more wheat around then. So even though wheat is selling for $4 a bushel when they make the contract, the contract price might be just $3 a bushel. Now, when the baker and the middleman determine a price for their contract with delivery next winter, they have to keep in mind that the next harvest might not be as good as the past one was, and perhaps by next winter there will be less wheat than there is now. So the price of wheat for next winter's delivery might be set at $4.50. As you can see, a lot of factors can influence the price of future contracts, and we'll discuss that later also. But the important point here is that although the price of future deliveries is related to the price of the current commodity, called the cash price or the basis, it is usually not going to be the same.

Of course, not everyone who trades commodities is a farmer, baker or middleman. Plenty of speculators go in and out of the market, but they are simply intermediaries in what is really a process of providing price security for the producer, the middleman and the ultimate user of the commodity. Now we'll look at how futures are traded on stock indexes and the changes which were made to accommodate the fact that there are differences between wheat (and other commodities) and stock indexes.

THE CONCEPT OF FUTURES ON STOCK INDEXES

The first obstacle one must overcome in trading stock indexes is a very natural aversion to risking money on something which doesn't exist. You can see a carload of wheat and you can smell a pork belly and you can heft a bar of silver. You can buy and sell stock because you get a nicely engraved certificate stating that you are the owner of so many shares. But what is a stock index? It doesn't exist except as a number you see in the newspaper financial pages. And how can there possibly be delivery of an average? What are they going to do? Give you one twentieth of a share of all seventeen hundred shares which comprise the Value Line Composite Average? That is absolutely preposterous. So one's first reaction to the entire concept of trading stock-index futures might be one of implausibility. It just can't be done. Well, it *is* being done, and in ever larger amounts every day, so let's look at how these apparent hurdles have been overcome.

First is the problem of trading something that doesn't exist, like the average of the prices of a lot of stocks. Let's go back to the concept of trading stocks. Yes, we know, stocks are real because you get a certificate stating that you own a part of a corporation, and that can be given a precise price. But just what is a corporation? Have you ever thought about that? Has anyone ever seen General Motors? Oh, yes, you have seen cars produced by GM, you may have seen some of their assembly plants or even their main buildings in Detroit, but those are only buildings they own. They are not General Motors Corporation itself. Ask a lawyer friend what a corporation really is. He will tell you that a corporation is a legal entity—it has existence only as a legal concept. It does not take up space, it is not tangible. It is just a legal fiction. But it is in every respect a fiction! Now, take a fiction, divide it up into millions of tiny parts and then start trading those fractions of a fiction and you will understand what trading stocks is really about.

The important point here is that you can trade almost anything as long as it is capable of being reduced to a precise price. Yes, we know that when you purchase a share of General Motors you will get a certificate stating that you own some shares, but this is not the shares themselves, only a legal recording of the fact. For proof, if those share certificates are destroyed by fire, the corporation will send you a new certificate. So you really bought a legal fiction.

Now, if people can trade legal fictions, why can't they trade another number which can be precisely determined? In fact, one can argue that it is easier to conceptualize how people can trade the average of a lot of stocks than it is to figure out how one determines a fair price for the legal fiction called a share of stock. Who knows what one share of stock is really worth? But determining the price of the stock indexes is a purely mathematical matter, which can be done to one one-hundredth of a point.

People can trade anything. They could trade futures on the exact population of the United States as determined by the census bureau at the end of each year, or the size of the federal debt, or the number of people killed each month in automobile accidents in the United States. In summary, the average price of a number of stocks is hardly any more abstract than the price of one share of stock, and we are all familiar with that. The average reflects an additional mathematical step, but it is certainly not fundamentally different.

DELIVERY OF STOCK FUTURES

Second, we come to the question of delivery. Remember that at the heart of the traditional commodity transaction was a desire to make a sale now with the price fixed now, for delivery at a future date. Here we come to a major departure from the traditional commodity transaction. There can be no delivery of stock index futures. So what happens at the end of the contract term?

As we mentioned before, every day you hold a futures contract your account is marked to the market. This means that it is treated as if you had closed out your contract at the final price of each day. So if you bought a September contract for $168 on Wednesday morning, and at the end of the day the contract closed at $169, your account would show a profit of $1, which is multiplied by $500 to give you a profit of $500 in your account. This is money you can withdraw, just as if you had bought stock and sold it at the end of the day for a $500 profit. Of course, you did not sell your futures contract, but your account is treated as if you had. The next day, if the contract goes up by 2 points, you will show an additional profit of $1,000. If it then goes down by $0.50, your account is reduced by $250. Thus, each day the actual cash in your account reflects the closing price of your futures contract. On the final day of the life of the contract it is adjusted to the closing price of the contract just as it has been every other day. The only difference is that the following day that futures contract will not appear on your statement. It has simply disappeared. This is true whether you are long or short the contract. Thus you can see that delivery has been replaced by a final marking to the market in the case of stock-index futures. This really makes so much sense, since we are talking about a financial future which involves only money. What better way to have delivery of money than to bring the account right up to date every day, so that on the final day there is no delivery necessary? This is not possible in the case of traditional commodities. How could you add a little wheat to your account every day? Not only is that impossible, but also it would defeat the basic purpose of the contract, which was to move that wheat at a specific price. But in the case of a purely financial transaction, like a stock-index future, there is no sense in moving around a lot of money.

It may make it easier for you to understand if you conceptualize that what stock-index futures trading comes down to is that you are not really buying or selling anything, you are simply taking a position in a contract at a fixed price. Instead of buying an actual commodity, you are simply fixing your entry price now. If the index moves up and you are long a contract, you will be credited with the difference. If you are short, you will be debited.

These changes in your account are made every day until the day of the expiration of your contract. Then they simply stop being made. It is as simple as that. No delivery is needed, because unlike the buyer of a wheat future, you do not want to get five thousand bushels of wheat. You only want to make money from an anticipated increase in the price of the index. You are simply undertaking a transaction based upon an average which is incapable of being delivered. But its changes in price are very capable of being measured, and by buying a future on this index you have said that you wish to participate in the increases or declines in the index. And that is what will happen every day.

MARGIN FOR STOCK-INDEX FUTURES

Since the basic concept of a commodity future is that nothing has taken place when the transaction was entered into except that the price was fixed, there is no need to pay the purchase price at that time. What you have done is assume a legal obligation to buy or sell something in the future. To assure your compliance with this obligation, you leave a good-faith deposit, and that is what is loosely called margin. This is quite different from buying stock on margin. In that case the margin is money you borrow from your brokerage firm and on which you pay interest. Here nothing is borrowed, and no interest is charged. As mentioned before, the current amounts required are $3,500 a contract for the NYSE, $6,000 for the S&P 500 and $6,500 for the VLCA. So if you want to get started with the smallest amount of money possible, then the NYSE is for you. Incidentally, these are the exchange minimums for speculators, and any brokerage firm is free to set higher requirements if it wishes.

If you can satisfy your brokerage that you are not engaged in stock-index trades as a speculator but rather as a hedger, you will qualify for greatly reduced margin requirements. A hedger uses the future to offset his risk from holding the underlying commodity. In this case if you owned a portfolio of diversified stocks worth at least the current price of one of the indexes multiplied by $500, you could qualify as a hedger for one contract. Thus if an index were at 130 and you owned at least $65,000 worth of stock and were going to short one futures contract, you might be able to qualify as a hedger. Note that this only works when you are trying to offset the risk of owning the stocks by going short the future. If you own all the stock in the world and want to go long one stock-index future, that would make you a speculator. The current margin requirements for hedgers at a typical brokerage firm are $1,500 for the NYSE, $2,500 for the S&P 500 and $3,250 for the VLCA.

There is a final, even lower requirement for spreaders. Later we will discuss spreading, which involves going long one future of an index and going short another. For example, you might go long the December VLCA and go short the March VLCA. Obviously your risk is much less than if you just buy or sell a position, so it stands to reason that your margin requirement should be less. The spread margin requirement for all index futures is $1,000. All figures given above are the exchange minimums, and individual brokerage firms are free to set higher requirements.

Using T Bills for Margin. For large traders the initial margin requirement can be fulfilled by supplying Treasury bills instead of cash. For purposes of providing margin these are valued at 90% of their value, so it takes $10,000 of T bills to give you $9,000 of margin. But the advantage is that you will be earning interest on the Treasury bills, whereas brokerage firms do not pay interest on the cash in commodity margin accounts. When interest rates are high, this is a very worthwhile method of picking up extra money.

MARGIN CALLS

So far we have discussed initial margin requirements. Unfortunately, this is only half the story. When a contract moves against you, you are required to pay in the loss at the end of any day that your margin sinks below the maintenance level. The maintenance level is 75% of the initial margin requirement—that is, for the NYSE it is $2,625, for the S&P 500 it is $4,500 and for the VLCA it is $4,875. As soon as the balance in your account falls below this level you will be required to add cash to your account, and you will have to send in enough to bring the account up to original maintenance. Let's take an example of how this works.

Assume that you believe the market will go up, and you buy a contract for 140 on the S&P 500. You bring in a check for $6,000 to meet the initial margin requirement. Assuming that the contract closes at your purchase price of 140, at the end of the day your account will show a credit balance of $6,000. This meets the initial margin requirement, so your account will show neither a margin call nor an excess. On the next day, assume that your contract closes down a full 3 points, at 137. Your account will now show an opening credit balance of $6,000 minus the loss that day of 3 times $500, or $1,500. Therefore at the end of the second day you will show a credit balance of $4,500. The maintenance requirement of 75% of $6,000 is exactly $4,500. So your balance is not below the maintenance requirement. Therefore there is no margin call, and there is no excess either.

The following day the market does pretty well in the morning, but then retreats in the afternoon, and your contract closes almost unchanged, down just $0.05, at 136.95. The loss is just .05 times $500, or $25. This reduces your credit balance to $4,475. Now you are below maintenance level. How much will your margin call be? $25? No. Once you fall below maintenance you must bring the account back up to the original margin requirements. Therefore you will get a margin call for $1,525 to bring it up to the original $6,000. Once you send this amount and it is credited to your account, then the entire process starts over again. If you do not meet the margin call, your broker will liquidate sufficient positions in your account to meet the call.

On the upside you can take out your winnings as they occur. In our example, you bought a contract for 140 and paid in $6,000. If the next day your contract closed at 141, then your account would be credited with a gain of $500. This would give you a credit balance of $6,500. Since the maximum margin requirement is the initial one, you would be able to take $500 from your account. In practice I would not recommend this, since there is such a good chance that within a very short time you might have to put it right back again if the contract moves against you.

Since large traders usually use Treasury bills for their initial margin, it is worth giving an example of the fact that they cannot be used for additional margin. Let's say you intend to trade a large number of contracts, so you purchase $100,000 worth of Treasury bills and place them in your commodity account. You start out small with just two contracts, requiring an initial margin of $12,000. They move against you, and you receive a maintenance call of $4,000. Indignantly you inform your broker that there is a surplus of $88,000 in your Treasury bill account, and you politely request that they take the money out of that account, perhaps by borrowing money against the Treasury bills instead of asking you to send in even more so that you have an even larger excess. Sorry. The regulations say that this cannot be done. You must send in the money.

An alternative is to sell some of the Treasury bills; then the money received from them can be used. Or you can keep some Treasury bills in your regular stock account with the same brokerage firm, and you can borrow against those. A cautionary note: Treasury bills in your stock account cannot be used for initial margin, and when you borrow against them you will pay interest to the brokerage firm on the amount you borrow. This interest cost will very likely be higher than the rate of return on the Treasury bills. A strategy hint: Keep enough Treasury bills in your commodity account to cover the initial margin requirements. Then have the maintenance calls come out of your stock account, where you can buy Treasury bills when you have a substantial excess, sell them when you have large house calls and borrow against the Treasury bills when you have relatively small margin calls.

LOSING MORE THAN YOUR MARGIN

Now that we understand just how commodity margin rules apply to stock-index futures, we can understand more fully the amount of risk we are undertaking by trading commodities. We've all heard stories of the person who started trading commodities with perhaps $10,000, then saw his commodity move against him by "the limit" every day for days so that he could not get out of his position, and he ended up with a loss of $50,000. This is not possible when trading stock-index futures because they do not have a daily limit, so you cannot be locked into a position. Nevertheless, there is always the possibility of losing more than you have invested. Here is one way it could happen.

Let's say you go long a contract on the NYSE, at 70, and you send in your maintenance margin of $3,500. On the second day the contract declines by 1.75 to 68.25, and your balance is reduced to $2,625. As we saw above, there is no margin call, since you just cover the maintenance margin requirement. But on the third day there is a real shake-out, and the contract falls 4 points, to 64.25. This means that your balance has fallen by $2,000, down to $625. A margin call goes out immediately at the end of day three to you for $2,875 to bring the account back to original margin requirement. You tell your broker that you will bring in the money the next day. On day four the contract falls another 2 points, so your account suffers another $1,000 loss, meaning that you now have a negative balance of $375. This means that you have lost $375 more than you originally invested. You are legally responsible for paying that amount.

This example illustrates two points. The first is the obvious one, that in unusually big market moves of two or more days in a row, you could lose more than you originally invested. But to anyone familiar with the movements of the NYSE Index this example shows that this will happen only in extreme situations. During the period January 1975 through March 1982, only once every two hundred trading days did the NYSE Index move more than 1.80. The futures contracts would in all likelihood move significantly more than the index itself, so there could be moves of 4 points, but they would probably happen less than once a year during an average year.

THE RISK IN MEETING MARGIN CALLS

Far more common than being locked in, but even more dangerous because it is more insidious, is to lose more money than you originally planned to invest because you continuously meet margin calls by bringing in more money. And before you say that you would never let yourself get in over your head, just think for a minute about how easy it is. In the first place, almost no one starts trading stock-index futures unless he has a fairly strong belief about which way the stock market is going to go. Deep in your heart you either know that the market is now about to go higher than it ever has in history, or that it is about to collapse. So you take your position in accordance with your belief. The position goes against you, and you receive a margin call. You have two choices. You can refuse the margin call and be sold out, or you can meet the call by sending in the money. Keep in mind that the first margin call will not be for an enormous sum, but probably for something just over 25% of what you originally put in. Thus if you started trading one NYSE contract for $3,500, the first margin call might be for about $950. If you do not send in the money, your position will be closed out; you will realize a loss of the amount of the margin call; and most importantly, you will be out of the position. It is the latter point which has the greatest impact.

Let's assume you went short. You went into the position originally because you believed that the index was going to go down. Since you put on that position, nothing has happened to make you change your mind. The federal deficit is still going to be the same, interest rates haven't changed appreciably, there has been no improvement in the economy or the forecasts. Therefore, why should you change your mind? And indeed, if you believed that the market was headed for a fall when you put on the position, now that the market is even higher than it was then, you are convinced that it has even farther to go on the downside. So by sending in less than $1,000 you have an opportunity to keep your investment alive, the chance to avoid taking any loss and above all the opportunity to have the market turn in your favor so that your unrealized loss is transformed into the big gain you *know* will occur.

They say on Wall Street that every speculator is driven by two basic forces: fear and greed. Here we see them both in action: fear that by not sending in the money you will realize an unnecessary loss, and that once you are out of the position the market will tumble down and you will be missing out on what should be your rightful profits; and greed, which is your basic motivation to make money, driving you to stay in there and risk more and more money.

The argument for not sending in any money and thus closing out the position is not as compelling. It is simply that by so doing you have limited your loss. So it should not be surprising that many people send in more money. And then perhaps the market will move in their favor for a little while, and then it may turn against them again. Once more they are faced with the same dilemma. And now, in addition to all the arguments given above for sending in more money is an additional one, namely the feeling that I have gone along with this for so long, and already put in so much money, that it would really be a shame to get out now and take such a large loss. Just a little bit more money and I may be able to save the entire situation and turn it from a near disaster into a gold mine.

In our chapters on strategies we will deal with this problem. Suffice for now to demonstrate how easily one can lose more than he originally puts in.

TERMINATING POSITIONS

There are two ways that a position can end. You can enter an offsetting transaction to close out the position by either selling out a long position or buying in a short position; or the position can expire.

A closing transaction is quite different from selling a stock, just as getting into a futures position was quite different. The big difference is that there is no change of money to represent the underlying value of the position. For example, let us say that you are long a VLCA March contract, which you then sell for 147. The value of this contract would be $500 times 147, or $73,500. Yet upon the sale you will not receive $73,500. All that will be credited to your account is the difference between 147 and the closing price yesterday. Thus the sale of a contract is no different than marking it to market at the end of any other day when you did not sell it.

For example, let us suppose that your contract closed at 146 yesterday, and your account had a credit of $8,000 in it. If you sell the contract for 147 today, that is a gain of one point, or $500. At the close today you would show a credit of $8,500 minus the commission. Similarly, if the contract went down a point on the day you sold it, so that you sold it for 145 when it closed at 146 yesterday, your account would reflect the decline by a point, and you would have a closing credit of $7,500. Thus the only difference on your statement between the day before and the day after the sale is that the position of being long one March VLCA contract would not appear. And, of course, the entire credit balance would now be free to be sent out or reinvested, since there is no longer any margin requirement.

The other way for a position to terminate is for the contract to come to the end of its life. When this happens it is treated exactly as if you had entered into a closing transaction, and your brokerage firm will even charge you the regular commission. It closes out the position for the final price of the underlying index, not the last price of the future. This is an important distinction. Up until that final day you have been following, and your commodity account has been reflecting, the price of your futures contract. And as we know, this can be either significantly higher or lower than the underlying index. For instance, when your contract closed at 147, the Value Line Composite Average itself might have been 146. And it is possible that the last trade of that contract could have been at 146.50. No matter. If the index closed at 146, that is the price at which you will be deemed to have closed out your position. This is an extremely fair principle, and it means that there is no point in large manipulators trying to influence the price of a contract on the final day, because it will not make any difference. A group of large manipulators might be able to cause a run or a squeeze on a contract, but they are powerless to move any of the stock indexes by even one decimal point. Since these prices are used on the termination of the contract, this assures that there will be no power plays of the type not unheard of in traditional commodities, where large investors may try literally to buy up a market.

FUTURES EXPIRATION DATES

Trading in the different contracts stops at different times. The last trading day for the Value Line Composite Average is the last business day of the month. The NYSE has its last trading day the day before the last business day of the month. Really a bit unusual is the S&P 500, which stops trading on the third Thursday of the contract month.

MARKET ORDERS

There are a number of different ways that you can enter your order to buy or sell a stock-index future. The easiest is to put in a market order either to buy or to sell. A market order must be executed immediately on the floor of the futures exchange at the best price available at that moment. You use this type of order when you want to make certain it will be executed immediately and when your concern for certainty of execution overpowers your concern for price. The reason for this is that when you place a market order, you cannot know in advance what your cost is going to be. Let's say your broker says the market seems to be going up and that his quote machine shows that the last contract sold for 125.70. (Incidentally, those used to the stock market will be disappointed to learn that your broker cannot get bid and asked prices on his machine, except at rare times.) So he does not know what the offering price of that contract is when he is talking with you. All he knows is that the last time a contract was sold, the price was 125.70. Now your order comes to the floor of the exchange.

You and your broker are both somewhat in the dark about what the situation on the floor is at that moment. Was that last price caused by someone wanting to sell a contract? If so, it was probably bought by a floor trader who was paying a low price in the belief that he could sell it out in a few minutes for a higher price when the next buy order came in. In that case, the last price was what is called the bid price, or the price at which you would sell a contract on a market order. But a buy order at the market will fetch a higher price, called the asking or offering price. Perhaps you will pay 125.75, or if the contract does not trade very often, 125.80.

On the other hand, that last price of 125.70 might have represented someone else like you who was buying a contract for himself, and then perhaps you can buy it at the same price. But even more important than who was buying on that last trade is how long ago the last trade was made and what has happened to the market since. If the last trade was ten minutes ago, and since then the underlying index of your contract has risen by $0.50, you should expect to pay about $0.50 more for your contract. It will work the same way on the way down.

With this kind of system there is room for feelings that you were treated unfairly. If the market is going up and the last trade was 144, you might be chagrined to find that when you bought the contract a few minutes later you paid 145. But that's what can happen. One bit of advice from experienced hands in the commodity game: Don't bother complaining to the exchange that you were cheated. If you put in a market order, your floor broker is obligated to get an immediate fill on the order, and he is supposed to search for the lowest price he can find, but if he sees only an offer a full point higher than the last trade, that is the price he is going to take.

LIMIT ORDERS

If you want more precision on the price you are going to pay or receive, you can place a limit order. This specifies the highest price at which you are willing to buy a contract, or the lowest price for which you are willing to sell a contract. For example, you could place an order to buy at 144.30 and know you would not pay more than that. A limit order can be placed at the current price of the contract; below the current price; or if the contract is rising, you might even want to place a limit order with a price a bit above the last trade price. The advantage of a limit order is that under no circumstances can a trade be made outside your limit. Thus if the last trade on your contract was 73.40 and you place a limit buy order at 73.20, you cannot get a report back that you bought the contract at 73.30. You could get a report for less than 73.20, on that rare chance that the contract gapped down after trading at 73.25, but you will never pay more than your limit.

Why then doesn't everyone always use limit orders and make the limit nice and low? The answer is that there is no assurance that a limit order will be executed. It will not be executed if there are no contracts for sale at the price of your limit. And there are more than a few stories on Wall Street of people who missed making fortunes because they entered limit orders which were just a hairsbreadth from becoming executed, when the market suddenly turned in the wrong direction. Let's say that when the contract was 73.40 you decide it is really cheap, and you want to buy, but you think there is still a small further decline left, so you enter a limit order at 73.20. The next trade is at 73.30, and then one at 73.25. Then an item hits the newstape that sends the market surging up. Will you now admit that you made a mistake in your limit order, and rush in to buy the contract at perhaps 100 cents higher? Maybe you should, but psychology plays strange tricks on people's minds, and the chances are very good that you will let your pride stand in the way and stick with your order, assuming the run-up is only temporary. And, of course, the higher the market goes, the less you will feel like admitting your error and paying an ever higher price.

A proper use of a limit order would be when the market is going against you and you decide you will increase your position at a more advantageous price. Let's suppose you went short a contract at 138.50. Now the contract has moved up, to 141.50. You still believe the contract will move down eventually and that this current rise in price presents an even better opportunity to short than when you did the original trade. So you tell yourself that if it goes up another point you will short another contract. If it does not, you will not be losing so much on the one you already sold and won't mind seeing the price go back down. So you place a limit order to sell one contract at 142.50. Whether the contract is executed or not, you have not suffered.

STOP-LOSS ORDERS
Another type of order is the stop-loss order. This is like the limit order, but instead of specifying that you want to sell a contract when it rises up to a certain price, you state that you want to sell a contract when the price declines to a stated price. For example, if a contract is now selling at 114, you might enter a stop-loss order to sell it at 112. Similarly, if a contract is now 170, you could enter a stop-order to buy it at 172. Why would anyone want to get worse prices than the going price for a contract? Stop-loss orders are used to protect against even greater losses if the contract declines farther. Let's assume the current price is 114 and you are long a contract because you believe that the long-term trend of the market is up. But you have enough experience to know that the short-term trend can be down and that it can be a vicious downturn, which could rob you of many more thousands of dollars than you care to lose. So even though you believe that in the long term the market will go up, what does that matter, when in the short term you could be wiped out? Remember the old military adage: He who fights and runs away lives to fight another day.

So you place your stop-loss order at 112 and hope that the order never goes off. But if the contract does trade at 112, then your order becomes a market order to sell. That means that it will be sold at the then best bid price available. So if the price is moving down in an orderly fashion, you should receive 112 or at least 111.95, but since you have a market order, there can be no assurance of what price you will actually get. In a really rapidly deteriorating market you might get only 111.90 or less.

The same rules apply to a stop-loss order on the buy side. You may be short a contract at 84 and believe firmly that the market is going to go down. But you also are enough of a realist to know that if you are wrong, the market could go up by 30 points if a major bull market develops. So you place a stop-loss order to buy in your contract if the price ever reaches 88. You hope that the market never does get that high, but if it does, you are willing to say "Uncle" and pack up your marbles and go home.

That covers the defensive uses of a stop-loss order. It also can be used to take on positions initially. For example, the market might be meandering in a tight range with no apparent direction. You study your charts and identify a breakout point. In other words, you say that if the market can ever rally above 127 on the index you are using, there could be an explosion on the upside. You compute that this would translate into a price of 130 on the contract month you are using. Now, you can either call your broker every hour and hope that you happen to call him at the very minute the contract crosses 130 (of course, taking the risk that the one day you can't call because you are on your office picnic is the day it bursts through), or you enter a stop-loss order to buy at 130 and just relax, knowing that your order will automatically be executed as a market order as soon as the contract trades at 130.

GOOD-TILL-CANCELED ORDERS
When an order is entered it is valid only for the day it is entered, unless it is marked as an open order or a GTC order, which stands for "good till canceled." In some cases you want an order to be good for one day only, but clearly in many of the limit order and stop-loss order situations we have discussed, you would want to place open orders. A GTC order remains valid until it is executed, or canceled by you, or the contract expires.

ONE ORDER CANCELS THE OTHER
In some strategies you will enter two orders, and when one order is executed, you want to cancel the other order. You can make sure that this is done automatically by using an OCO order, meaning "one cancels the other." This can be used only when both orders are on the same side—for example, when you have a sell order at a limit such as 152, and a sell order at a stop, such as 148.

It cannot be used when you have a sell order at a stop-loss position, and also a buy-stop order if it goes up, as, for example, when you are trying to pyramid your profits. If you cannot use an OCO order, make sure your broker understands that he should cancel the other order as soon as he knows that the one is executed. Your broker is probably not willing to guarantee that he will do this; it is important for you to get the reports of your executions promptly so you can instruct your broker to cancel the other order.

SELECTING THE EXPIRATION DATE

Once you have decided to get into stock-index futures trading and have selected which index you want to trade, the next step is to decide which month's contract you wish to buy or sell. The S&P 500 and VLCA will offer you the next four expirations, whereas the NYSE offers six. Since there is no actual delivery of anything in stock-index futures, you have a great deal of freedom in choosing which month you want to trade. Obviously, if you intend to be in the market for a long period without doing any trading, you are best served by going into a long-term contract. This saves you the expense of getting out of your short-term contract, paying a commission, and then having to get into a longer one. And each time you trade, you are probably losing $0.05 to $0.25 because you sell at the bid price and buy at the asking price. So, all things being equal, you would want to get the long-term contract.

One disadvantage of long-term contracts is that there is very little liquidity in them. In fact, that is an understatement with respect to the farthest-out contracts, which might not trade for days at a time. This means that the spread between the bid and the asked price is enormous. Thus you could buy a contract for 112, and if you decide to sell the next minute with no change in the underlying index, you might get no more than 110. That's a $1,000 loss, whereas if you had been in the near-term contract you might lose $0.10, equal to $50, or less. If you have absolutely no intention of getting out of the contract until the contract expires, then a long-term contract might be appropriate, but remember that a lot can happen in a year, and circumstances might well arise in which you would want to get out.

If you do decide to go into a near-expiration contract and then wish to continue the position when it is about to expire, it is fairly easy to close out that position and go into the next one. The commission isn't so large, and the difference in prices between the contract you are getting out of and the one you are getting into may be slight.

The primary factor affecting your decision of which contract to get into will be the price of the various expirations. In general the prices of the contracts go higher as the durations lengthen. The amount by which the price of any futures contract exceeds the price of the underlying index is called the premium. The longer-term futures tend to have higher premiums. Thus, if you are buying a future, you would be inclined to get a short-term contract and pay a lower price.

The offset is that when your contract expires, you will have to "roll out" to the next expiration by selling your contract and buying the next one. The next one will cost more than the one you are selling, and the combined premiums of the original cost to you of your shorter-term contract plus the premium and commissions you pay to roll out might exceed the cost of the premium if you had bought the longer-term contract in the first place.

If September is 134, and December is 136 when the index is 131, you are paying a $3 premium when you buy September, or a $5 premium on the December. When the September contract expires, assuming the index is still 131, the December contract may well be at 134. Thus if you bought the September and rolled out to December you will pay a total premium of $6, whereas you would have paid only $5 if you had bought the December in the first place.

THE EFFECT OF LOST INTEREST ON PRICES

The pricing at the various expiration months is very important, because it can tell us a lot about how the "average" of stock-index futures traders view the probable future course of the market. To understand what these prices mean, we must first understand what the prices should be under normal circumstances. By normal circumstances we mean there is no consensus about the future direction of the stock market.

Under normal times such as that, the prices of the various futures expirations should be determined by the interest cost savings which a purchaser of a portfolio of stocks would save by going long a future contract instead of actually buying the stocks. Let's assume that an index is at 110. Multiplying this by $500, we see that the value of that index is $55,000. Let us assume that someone is bullish on the stock market and decides to purchase $55,000 worth of stock. The money he has paid for the stock can no longer earn him interest, so he has a cost in the form of lost interest when he buys the stock. That cost is determined by looking at the interest he would receive in a completely risk-free investment, such as short-term Treasury bills. Let's assume that the current rate of three-month T bills is 10%.

Our hypothetical purchaser wants to speculate for six months. If he buys stock for six months, he is losing the interest on $55,000 at 10%, which is $5,500. For six months that is half of that, or $2,750. However, his net cost actually is less, since he will presumably be getting dividends from the stocks. If the stocks are paying 5%, then he would receive half of this cost from the dividends, so that his actual cost in interest is $1,375.

When he goes long a six-month stock-index futures contract, he has no interest cost. His margin cost, the original margin, equal to about 10% of the value of the index, times $500, can be in the form of T bills, which will earn money. He can do what he wishes with the 90% balance. If he puts it into T bills it is also earning interest. Therefore, by going long a stock-index futures contract, the speculator is saving himself the full interest cost of owning $55,000 of stock for six months.

In theory, this savings of $1,375 should be reflected in the price of the six-month contract. To determine just how this affects the contract price, divide $1,375 by 500. Here the result is that the six-month contract should theoretically be selling for 2.75 above the index and the one-year contract should be selling for 5.50 above the contract.

Notice that I have carefully said "should" be selling for that price and "theoretically" would be at that price. The reason is very simple. In the real world it has become clear that while these interest rates will have an effect on the futures prices, they are not the sole determinant, nor in most cases even the main one.

MARKET EXPECTATIONS

It has become clear that the expectations of investors are what influence the prices of the futures and are what give them their enormous volatility. When traders in stock-index futures believe that the market is headed up, then the prices of the futures greatly exceed the price of the underlying index, and when the stock-index-futures traders believe that the market is heading down, then the prices can be substantially below the index. This can be easily explained.

When the market is heading up, that means investors are more interested in buying stocks than they are in selling, and they are optimistic about the future of stock prices. It stands to reason that traders in the stock-index futures will have the same expectations. So more of them are interested in buying the contracts than in selling. As the buy orders pour in, the price of the futures go up. Similarly, in bearish times, when the market is low and is heading down, most investors tend to believe that it will continue to go down. So they short the stock-index futures. And there is a further source of selling from investors who maintain stock portfolios and want to hedge them against future declines in the stock market. The combined force of these selling orders can outweigh that of the buy orders, so that the price of the future goes substantially below the current price of the index itself.

PRICE OF FUTURES VS. THE INDEX

In the brief history stock-index futures have had, it is difficult to come up with what is the average and what is the extreme degree of over- or underpricing. The "average" price should be the theoretical price we discussed, which means that the future prices sell at a premium to the index in accordance with interest rates. In gloomy times the amount by which the futures can sell below the index can be surprisingly great. The largest difference of which I am aware occurred in the VLCA on June 18, 1982. At that time the Value Line Composite Average closed at 118, and the September 1982 contract settled at 112.90. Thus it was a full 5.10 points below the index. On the upside, the highest difference seems to be about 4 points on the VLCA.

The ramifications for the trader are extremely significant. If you believed that the market was going down, as so many traders obviously did on June 18, 1982, and you sold that September 1982 futures at 5.10 points below the index, look at what you were doing. You were speculating that the index would fall by more than 5.10 points, assuming that you intended to hold the contract position until expiration, and this assumption had to become true before you could even break even! That's a big handicap to overcome. But most of us are not long-term holders, and we are typically expecting to get out of our positions within a few weeks or less. What is the significance of this to us?

We know that the normal future price is above the index and that a discount from the index of 5 points is so low that it is very likely to correct itself in the near future. We can say that either the market must continue a rapid decline so that more and more people want to short the future, or else the price of the future will come up to or over the level of the index itself. What happened was that the market continued to fluctuate, but the September contract really never got much below 113. By August 18, 1982 the VLCA was back to 118 and the September was 117.60, just barely below the index. People who shorted the September contract on June 18 and then closed out their positions on August 18 really weren't wrong on which way the market would go, since the market stayed the same. But they were dead wrong on the discount which the future sold in relationship to the index. In fact, they lost 4.70 points, or $2,350 per contract. On the other hand, anyone who went long a contract on June 18, 1982 and sold out on August 18 wasn't right either. He thought that the market would go up, and it didn't. But look at his result. Yes. For not being right he did pretty well. He made $2,350 per contract.

FLUCTUATIONS OF PREMIUMS

The relationship of the futures price to the price of the underlying index is extremely important. In the first place, it gives you a very clear picture of the overall sentiment of the futures at that very moment. If the indexes rise more than the futures prices, that means that futures traders, on the average, do not believe the rally will last. If the indexes are down and the futures are not down by as much, it means they believe the decline is only minor and that the market will soon snap back. Most of the time, however, any major move will be exaggerated by the futures. Typically, if an index makes a good solid move upward—by, say, 2 or more points—you will find that the futures move up by one and a half times that amount. The newspaper will often show that the index is up 3 points, and the futures are up 4.50 points.

That level of the futures, however, poses a problem for those who are long, because the futures action yesterday has anticipated a continuing rally today. That is obvious because compared to the closing prices the day before, the premium of the futures price is 1.50 points higher than it was. This is the market's way of saying that the futures traders believe there will be a 1.50-point rally in the very near future. What happens next is often a puzzle to novices.

There are three possibilities. First, the index could go up by about 1.50 points. If it goes up by 1.50 points, do not be surprised if the futures contract does not move. Thousands of people will be calling their brokers after the rally and exclaiming, "I don't understand it! The world is against me! How can it be that I buy the futures at the closing price yesterday, then the index goes up a full 1.50 points and the futures don't even move?" The answer is that when this person bought his futures contract, it already had a price increase of 1,50 points built into it, anticipated by the market. The price he paid already included a 1.50-point rally the next day. When it happened, the futures price was already right in place.

A second possibility is that the index might go up by more than 1.50 points. Then the futures price is likely to continue its rise, because in an up market, the futures tend to command an increasing premium over the index price. Therefore, if the index moved up 3 points, the futures could easily move up by 3 points, or even 4. Not only would it go up to reflect the increase in the index, but also it would probably increase the premium over the index.

The third possibility is that the index goes up by less than 1.50 points. Now the extra 1.50-point premium built in yesterday turns out to be incorrect—that is, the premium built in yesterday reflected the futures traders' aggregate belief that the rally would continue into today. But if that rally does not continue, then the premium should not exist. And that is just what will very likely happen. If the index remains unchanged for a while, the futures are very likely to fall by those 1.50 points, or a good portion of it, so that the relative price of the futures and the index are back to where they were before yesterday's moves. Once again, a thousand new stock-index-futures traders are going to be surprised and disappointed. "But why is my futures contract down by 1.50 points when the index itself is unchanged? Shouldn't the futures have the same price too?"

From these three examples we can draw some conclusions. If there is a strong day in the market, the futures tend to outperform the indexes. If there is no follow-through the next day, the futures will fall back, and their relationships to the index will revert to what they were before. If, however, there is a continuing strong price action in the same direction, then the premium over the index will increase. And, of course, everything said here works in reverse when prices decline. If there is a 3-point decline, the futures will very likely fall by 4 points. If the next day the index stays the same, watch for the futures to go back up by a point or so. What all of this comes down to is that the futures movements tend, over the very short period, to exaggerate the movement of the index. But once large moves are completed, the futures tend to go back to the relationship they had with the index.

BENEFITING FROM FUTURES PRICES

What this means to thoughtful traders is that when the futures are selling at a large premium over the index, the odds favor the short seller, because not only must that premium disappear between now and the expiration date of the contract, but in the short run there is also a good chance that once the indexes stop moving up, that premium will disappear. When the futures are selling at a hefty discount to the index, then the odds favor the buyer of the futures for the same reasons.

Although these rules seem simple to apply, they are *not*. When the premiums are high, it is because most people believe that now at last the market is in for a really big move up. And you will probably think so too. Nevertheless, if you will wait perhaps as little as two hours, it can sometimes pay off in moves of 2 points in a futures price. Certainly when I see that yesterday the index was up by 3 points and the futures were up by 5 points I would not rush in to buy at yesterday's closing price.

It is not true that the public is always wrong. But as Harry Brown once said, if you always go with the public, you just won't ever make very much money. This is because when the public is wrong, you are going to lose. But even when they are right, the prices will already reflect to a large degree the public's belief of what is going to happen. For example, if the market roars up and everyone believes this is the start of the next great ten-year bull market, the futures are going to rise by far more than the index. You step up to buy a futures contract, and it already has built into its price the expectation of a good rally for the next few days. If the market does have a rally but it is nothing sensational, you may not make any money at all. If the market stays flat or goes down, you will suffer very large losses. Only if the market continues to make steep advances in the near future will your position work out. So you can figure that the odds are against you. You have about four chances to lose, and only one chance in five to make any money. Of such things are the sheep separated from the wolves on Wall Street.

STOCK FUTURES ARBITRAGE

Since the differences between the underlying stock indexes and the prices of the futures are so important, it is worth spending some time on that topic. At first it might seem that the spreads would become extremely wide. After all, when the market is going down, everyone wants to hedge his long stock position by selling the futures short, and at the same time that is when most successful traders figure that the market will continue its trend of going down. Who is going to buy? Given a large enough discount to the price of the index, there will always be someone to buy. But, fortunately, there is an even better reason why that spread should not get too great. This is that some of the firms on Wall Street which engage in arbitrage have begun to arbitrage the futures.

Arbitrage consists in buying and simultaneously selling essentially similar securities. The classic case in the days before telegraphs was to buy New York Central stock, for example, in New York at a low price on sudden bad news, then send a courier racing on horseback to Philadelphia to sell the same stock there at a higher price before they heard the news. And you thought that those pony express riders just did it for the sport! In any event, it is possible for an arbitrageur, with the help of a computer, to make up a portfolio of fifty or so stocks which, based upon their past history, will move almost exactly the same way as one of the indexes. In effect, the firms can create their own index funds which ought to mirror the movement of the index they are trying to duplicate. Now, let us say that a tremendous wave of bullishness hits the market. Speculators start buying up stock index futures like crazy, and at the same time all those who had previously been short start to panic, and they begin to buy the futures contracts too. In short, there are very few sellers left and a large number of buyers, so one result is that the six-month futures go to a premium of 5 points above the index.

Enter the arbitrageur. He will sell the contract for 5 points above the index, then purchase those carefully selected groups of stocks which will essentially mirror the index. At the expiration of the futures contract, he buys it in and sells the stocks. Result: Whether the index goes up or down, the arbitrageur will capture those 5 points. At the present time we cannot know whether the index will move up or down in the future, but we do know that at the expiration date of the contract it will be at exactly the same price as the index. Since the arbitrageur is short the contract and long its equivalent, whether the market moves up or down, he will gain those 5 points. Thus, the greater the premium of the futures contract becomes, the more incentive there is for the arbitrageurs to step in and sell the futures. This selling will tend to keep the premiums within bounds.

When the world is bearish and everyone is shorting the contracts to hedge their long positions or just to make money from what they figure is the coming collapse of the stock market, the futures will fall to a substantial discount below the index. Here the arbitrageur steps in again, this time doing just the opposite. He buys the futures contract at a bargain and sells the stock selection short. Hence he is locking in the difference again, and he will gain the amount of the discount regardless of whether the market goes up or down.

Incidentally, it is virtually impossible for anyone but an arbitrage firm to do this because commissions on the stock would be very large, and the margin required to buy or to short the stock would also be very high. But remember that member firms of the stock exchanges and the futures exchanges do not have to pay commissions on their own purchases, and that when they buy or sell stock short, the margin is a small fraction of what you or I must pay. In fact, when a member firm sells stock short, it gets to keep the money it takes in from the sale, and it can invest this money on a short-term basis to earn interest from it. So a firm can actually short a selection of stocks, buy a futures contract and make money from the interest. This means that the futures contract doesn't need to get to a very steep discount from the index for it to pay for the arbitrageurs to come in. Therefore we may never again see such large discounts as were available in the first year of the stock-index market, now that the arbitrageurs have discovered stock-index futures.

COMMISSIONS

As in all commodities trading, there is no commission charged on the opening transaction for a stock-index future, whether you are buying a contract to go long or selling one to go short. The commission is charged only on the closing transaction. If you terminate your position in a contract by allowing it to expire, that will be treated as a closing transaction and you will be charged a commission upon the expiration.

Each brokerage firm is allowed to set its own commission rates. A typical rate is $85, althought if a firm is not a member of the exchange on which the futures are being traded, it may charge $100 or more. This is the rate for regular trades, where you open the transaction on one day and sell it on another. If you open and close the transaction on the same day, which is called day trading, then the commission is usually reduced. A typical rate for a day trade would be $55. There are also special rates for spreads, and a typical spread commission might be $45 for each side of the spread.

Clearly there is a dramatic savings in commissions on day trades vs. overnight trades. And brokerage firms are pleased to give you this discount because they believe that it encourages traders to trade more often. In fact, your brokerage firm may give you the benefit of the day-trade discount commission even when you don't think you deserve it. Here's an example.

Let's say that on Monday you go long a contract at 150. On Thursday morning the contract has appreciated to 155, and you decide to take your profit and sell it out at that price. No overnight trade there. Shortly thereafter the market suddenly begins to go down. By late afternoon the contract you sold in the morning has fallen to 152, and you decide to go back on in. You buy the contract to establish a new opening position. To you this is clearly the opening of another long position.

The brokerage firm, however, looks at these trades differently. In fact, of course, there is a computer looking at these trades and calculating the proper commission. The computer sees a purchase of a contract at 152 and a sale of the same contract at 150, both done on the same day. To the computer, this is a day trade. Don't complain! You will be happy to learn that you will be given the day-trade rate on these trades even though as far as you are concerned, there was no day trade at all.

The fact that the computer connected the closing trade of one position with the opening trade of another position causes an interesting side effect, which can lead to unnecessary confusion unless you understand what has happened. In your mind, the sale on Thursday morning was of the contract you had purchased on Monday and resulted in a profit of 5 points, or $2,500. The purchase at 152 opened up another long position. Thus, at the close of business on Thursday, you concluded that you had realized a profit of $2,500 and had a new position with a cost basis of 152. That's not how your brokerage firm sees it!

Since the brokerage firm paired up the two trades on Thursday, it reports things accordingly. As far as they are concerned, you purchased a contract on Monday at 150, and then on Thursday you sold a new contract for 155 and purchased it back for 152. If it were not the same contract, you would not have done a day trade. But since you did do a day trade, and of course you do want to make the commission savings of a day trade, it had to be the same contract which was purchased and sold on Thursday. Therefore, your sale on Thursday at 155 and purchase at 152 resulted in a profit of 3 points, or $1,500. This is what will show up on your monthly statement as a realized gain. By the same token, the contract you purchased on Monday has not been affected by the trades on Thursday. So you finish the day on Thursday long your original contract, with a cost to you of 150. If the settlement price is 152, then you will have an unrealized profit of 2 points. It all works out exactly the same in the end, but it can lead to differences if you ask your broker how much money you made on Thursday and what the cost of the contract is that you are long on Friday.

Those used to paying commissions on stock and options will find that these commissions are very low. For instance, if you are charged $75 for trading an S&P 500 contract and you must deposit a margin of $6,000, that comes to just 1.25%. On options, commissions typically rang from 4% to 9%. Furthermore, remember that futures commissions are charged only on closing trades. If it were allocated to both parts of the trade, like commissions on stocks or options, it would be just half that, or only 0.625%. But it really becomes a bargain if you think of what is behind the $6,000 margin you are depositing. Yes, what about the fact that you control approximately $75,000 worth of stock with that contract? Can you imagine buying and then selling $75,000 worth of stock, all for a total commission of just $75? Why, you would be lucky to get away with a commission of under $1,000 for the buy alone! The low commission is indeed a reason why it makes sense for many people who were trading stocks or options to switch to index futures.

In calculating your profits and losses you must always subtract the commission on the closing positions. But because the commission amount varies with different brokerage firms, and to simplify matters, they have not been deducted from the examples in the rest of this book. If you really want to be accurate, subtract the commission amount your brokerage firm charges you from each example.

FOLLOWING THE DAILY REPORTS

One of the big advantages of dealing in stock-index futures is that it is so much easier to follow the price of one futures contract rather than a number of individual stocks. The prices are listed in newspapers in the section on commodities or futures prices. In most newspapers, these prices are divided into different types of futures, and stock-index futures are listed under "Financial." Since *The Wall Street Journal* is a national publication, we will use it here as our example (see Figure 1).

Let's start with the S&P 500. "CME" means that it is traded on the Chicago Mercantile Exchange. The "500 times index" means that the actual value of each contract is $500 multiplied by the price of the futures contract. The first line here is for the March 1983 contract. Each of the columns is labeled toward the top of the figure. The first

Futures Prices

Thursday, February 3, 1983
Open Interest Reflects Previous Trading Day.

— FINANCIAL —

	Open	High	Low	Settle	Change	Lifetime High	Lifetime Low	Open Interest
S&P 500 FUTURES INDEX (CME) 500 Times Index								
Mar83	143.95	145.90	143.80	144.90	+ .85	150.85	101.85	14,707
June	144.90	146.70	144.70	145.80	+ .85	151.65	102.50	1,621
Sept	145.90	147.30	145.30	146.40	+ .80	152.10	120.70	74
Dec	146.75	148.00	146.10	147.00	+ .80	152.60	138.00	171

Est vol 26,988; vol Wed 27,881; open int 16,573, +362.

S&P 500 STOCK INDEX (Prelim)

143.59 144.43 143.25 144.27 + 1.04

NYSE COMPOSITE FUTURES (NYFE) 500 Times Index								
Mar83	83.05	84.20	83.00	83.60	+ .45	87.15	58.45	4,417
June	83.65	84.70	83.55	84.15	+ .45	87.75	59.25	941
Sept	84.60	85.15	84.50	84.70	+ .45	87.80	59.65	606
Dec	85.00	85.00	85.00	85.25	+ .45	88.20	60.88	251
Mar	85.40	85.40	85.40	85.80	+ .45	89.00	79.25	91
June	....	....	....	86.35	+ .45	89.00	82.30	34

Est vol 11,503; vol Wed 11,747; open int 6,340, −171.

NYSE COMPOSITE STOCK INDEX

82.62 83.35 82.62 83.26 + .59

KC VALUE LINE FUTURES (KC) 500 Times Index								
Mar83	167.00	169.35	167.70	167.90	+ .70	173.40	110.:0	2,202
June	168.10	170.10	167.65	168.90	+ .80	174.30	111.00	426
Sept	169.10	170.40	169.10	169.70	+ .80	175.00	111.35	416
Dec	169.70	171.20	169.70	170.50	+ .80	175.50	111.40	142
Mar	....	....	....	171.40	+ .80	176.50	161.65	4

Est vol 3,524; vol Wed 3,469; open int 3,190, +244.

KC VALUE LINE COMPOSITE INDEX

165.54 166.63 165.54 166.56 + 1.02 ....

Figure 1

price listed here, 143.95, was the opening price, or the price at which the first trade of the day took place. This would be important if you had placed a market order before the opening. The price you receive should be this price, although sometimes there are two or more opening prices, called split openings. Next comes the high for the day, here 145.90. This would be particularly important if you were trying to sell your contract at a certain price. Let's say you had an order in during the entire day to sell your September S&P 500 contract for 145.75. You look at the second column and see that the high for the day was 145.90. Since this is above your limit, you must have sold your contract for 145.75. If the high for the day was 145.75, this would not indicate that you necessarily sold your contract, since there might have been a number of contracts for sale at that price, and only a few of the ones offered for sale were actually sold at that level. But if the high for the day is higher than your limit, then you should have sold it. (Another use for the high price for the day is to make sure you did not pay more than the high for the day.) Incidentally, this is a good time to point out that you should always check the confirmation statements from your brokerage firm. Mistakes do happen, and it is very easy for a figure to get transposed, or misread by a busy clerk. So in addition to checking with your broker about the transaction prices, carefully check the written statements from your firm to be sure that everything works out.

The next column is the low for the day. This is important if you were trying to buy a contract for a limit price, or to make sure that if you sold a contract you didn't get less than you should have. The next column is headed "Settle" (or "Close" in some newspapers), and reports the settlement price, which is equivalent to the closing price in the stock market. The reason it is not called "Close" is that the exchange officials may not use the actual last price if they believe it does not reflect the real value of that contract at the close. The most common reason for that would be if one of the contracts does not trade very often. If the last trade were twenty minutes before the close, and just after that some very bullish news came out so that all the other contracts went up by about $0.50, to print the last trade in the paper would lead everyone to believe that this one contract was a real bargain, when of course it just didn't trade after the market went up. So the exchange officials would make up a figure which they believe represents the price the contract would have traded at the close if there had been a trade then.

The settlement price is the most useful of the prices, because it is the final price of the day, which tells you what is most likely to happen on the next day, and it is the one used to compute your profit or loss and your margin requirements. The column headed "Change" tells you the direction and amount of change in today's settlement price from yesterday's settlement price.

"Lifetime (or Season) High and Low" tells you the highest price and the lowest price at which this contract has ever traded. Do not be misled by the fact that the prices for the nearest-term contract will probably have the biggest swing from lifetime high to lifetime low. That is because it has had a much longer lifetime and does not mean it is more volatile than the others. The longest-out contract may have been in existence for only a few weeks, so naturally it has not had time to go from a very high level to a very low one.

A word of caution: When you look at these life-of-the-contract highs and lows it is a great temptation to use them as limits. For example, here the life-of-the-contract low was 101.85, and if you are going long the contract, you might say to yourself that it can go down only another 13 points. Obviously this is not true. Highs and lows merely indicate where the contract happened to be in the past and have nothing to do with where it will go in the future. Life-of-the-contract highs and lows are broken frequently, particularly in a young market such as this. And if you are short a contract and it goes through its lifetime high, that is when the shorts really start to worry. Not only does the previous life-of-the-contract high not provide you with any protection, but also there is a common view that once a contract breaks one of these limits it is even more likely to go much farther in the same direction.

Open Interest. The final figure listed is the open interest. This represents the number of contracts currently outstanding, the number in existence. While this may seem straightforward, it is not quite as easy a concept as it first appears. Compare the open interest in a futures to the number of shares of stock outstanding. Initially a corporation issues a fixed number of shares. Since a corporation may neither issue any more shares nor buy in any of its shares, the number of outstanding shares can remain exactly the same year after year. Futures contracts are quite different because they are not issued by a corporation. Rather, every time someone sells a contract short as part of an opening transaction and that contract is bought by someone going long as an opening transaction, then a contract has literally been created, and the open interest has been increased by one. That is to say, there is now one more contract in existence than there was before, and the open interest figure is one higher than it was before.

There are a lot of trades, however, which do not result in any increase in the open position. For example, let us assume that a person is short a contract. During the day someone else decides to sell one contract short as an opening transaction. At the same time our speculator decides that he will close out his position by buying a contract. So he buys the contract to close out his position which the other trader sold to open his position. The result is that there has been no change in the open position. Our man reduced the open position by closing out his short position, but someone else created a position by initiating a short trade. Another way of looking at this is that the short position was simply sold from one person to another, without any increase in the open position tally.

Estimating Volume. Thus we can see that the open position is not directly tied in with the volume. There can in fact be thousands of trades, and if the number of contracts which are opening positions is equal to the number of contracts traded which are closing positions, there will be no increase in the open position. Notice that the open position is invariably the largest in the nearest-term contract, except when it has only a few days left, and then the next shortest duration will be the largest. The size of the open position generally declines rapidly for the farther-out expiration periods. This does not mean that there is almost no volume in the contract, because, as we have seen, there can be a lot of buying and selling every day but no increase in the open position. Unfortunately, the actual volume of trades in any contract is not published, and it is not even readily available to your broker. Therefore we have to assume that the larger the open position, the more trading there is. And this is important because the greater the volume, the greater the liquidity in the contract. By liquidity we mean the ability to buy or sell a quantity of contracts at a price the same as or very close to the last price. This in turn helps determine how readily you can make rapid trades for a profit on a small change in the futures price.

For example, if a contract just traded at 137.50 and you want to buy ten contracts, you could put in a limit order for, say, 137.50, but you run the risk that in the few minutes it takes for your order to get to the floor and be executed, the market might have moved up and you will miss your order, to your later disadvantage. A higher limit, such as 137.55 or 137.60, runs the risk that the market will have declined in the time it takes to get your order to the floor, and your order will be filled at your limit, which is still more than you ought to pay. The ideal would be if you knew there was enough activity going on, so that at all times there were brokers actively competing to sell contracts at the lowest possible price. If this were the case you could simply place an order at the market and be confident that the price you paid really was the lowest reasonable price at that time. Obviously, if a contract is being bought and sold in large quantities every minute, there must be a lot of brokers competing on the floor, and they are going to have to offer a low price to get the order from your broker. On the other hand, if only a few contracts change hands during an entire day, this means that there is not enough business to attract more than one or two brokers, and they can mark up the contracts they are selling by a higher amount.

A second reason why volume is significant in addition to the competition for a large number of brokers is that if a floor broker knows that due to the large volume he will be able to buy from someone else very soon the contract which he just sold to you, he will not need such a large markup to protect him from adverse changes in the market. If a contract trades only once an hour, on the other hand, then he is entitled to take a bigger markup because he must hold the contract for a period during which the market could move against him. Thus, in summary, the bigger the open position, the more liquid we can assume the market for that issue to be. The conclusion is that where you see a large open position, such as a few thousand contracts and more, you can enter market orders with a fair degree of safety. But where the open interest is low, be forewarned that a market order is very likely to be filled at a price disadvantageous to you.

At the bottom of the report for each index is the total volume done that day, which as mentioned is not broken out as to the different months. The estimated volume is given for that day, and then the actual volume for the previous day. The total open interest is given for all the expiration months, and the change in this total interest.

Price of the Index. In *The Wall Street Journal*, as shown here, the last line for that index provides information about the underlying index itself. It gives the opening price of the index; its high, low and settlement price; and the amount of change. The importance of this is that by comparing the change in the index with the change in the contract you are interested in, you can determine whether the difference in price between your futures contract and the underlying index has increased or decreased. The report tells us that the S&P 500 Index closed up 1.04. The March contract closed up .85, meaning that the premium on the March contract decreased by $0.19.

For short-term traders, the differences in the moves between the index and the futures can be the most useful of the information displayed in the newspaper reports, since one of the simplest trading strategies is to short when the futures prices get significantly above the index and to buy when they are equal to or below the index.

OPENING A COMMODITIES ACCOUNT

Almost anyone can open a regular brokerage firm account to trade in stocks. Why not? If you have the money to buy a hundred shares of International Widgets of the World and you tell a broker you want to buy them, who will care if you buy them and there is a loss? You initiated the transaction, you selected the stock and if it goes down to zero you have no one to blame but yourself. Certainly the brokerage firm played almost no role in the transaction except to follow your orders, so it is hard to say that they should share responsibility. Your loss is limited to the amount of money you put up, and rarely do stocks drop to zero. When they do, it usually takes a long time, so you would have many weeks to sell out and limit your loss. In commodities everything is quite different.

In the first place, your cost of entry is just that small good-faith deposit, which in the case of stock-index futures amounts to about 10% of the index value. This means that a dramatic move in the market could wipe out your entire investment in just a few business days, as it would have had you gone short, for example, in late August 1982. (Remember when the Dow Jones went up 39 points in one day?) Second, it is very possible for you to lose more than you put up, as we demonstrated earlier. This means that the brokerage firm might be left with a debit in your account even after they liquidate your position. This means that they would have to try to collect the money from you (or absorb the loss themselves). No brokerage firm is interested in this type of possibility. Finally, there is much more communication between a typical commodities broker and his customer than there is with the typical stockbroker. This means that if there is a loss, much more of the burden is going to rest on the shoulders of the broker, which means that the brokerage firm itself may be ultimately responsible.

What all this comes down to is that a commodities account is not appropriate for everyone. In the words of Wall Street, a certain "suitability standard" determines who is allowed to open a commodities account. While the brokerage firms are certainly trying to get commissions from as many commodities customers as they can, they would rather not get commissions from someone who could be losing his lifetime savings, or the money he has earmarked for his child's tuition this year. Not only would this be bad for the firm's reputation, but also in some instances (not unknown), the customer might try to sue the firm.

FINANCIAL REQUIREMENTS
FOR A COMMODITIES ACCOUNT

Thus every brokerage firm has certain suitability standards to determine who can open a commodities account, and once that account is opened, just how deeply the customer can get involved. One major brokerage firm recommends that to participate in one of their financial futures programs you have a net worth of over $300,000 exclusive of the value of your home, and at least $60,000 of risk capital. This is quite high by industry standards and is not an indication of what is required to open an account and trade one contract. Typically a brokerage firm wants to see a net worth excluding your home of at least $75,000 and risk capital of $15,000 plus annual income of at least $40,000 to open the account. But all this is somewhat variable. For example, if you are young, that counts in your favor. The reason is not that anyone is discriminating against older people but rather that if you are young the assumption is that if you lose a substantial amount of your capital, you will have plenty of time left to earn more to replace it, whereas a retired person would find it impossible to recoup his losses. Also, a person still working in his sixties might have a large net worth, but that money would be earmarked for his retirement expenses, and if it were lost, he would have no way to replace his lifetime savings.

A second factor is the number of dependents. If you are a husband and sole support of a wife and three children, you are going to need more money than if you are single and supporting no one else.

Commodity Credit Limits. Once the account is opened, someone within the brokerage firm (but not your broker) will decide upon the credit limit you are entitled to. This is a limit on the size position you can have and is separate and in addition to the margin requirements. This limit may be in the form of the number of contracts you are allowed to be long or short in your account at any time, or it may be a dollar amount of your maximum margin requirement. These credit limits range all the way from two contracts for a retired man who indicates assets of about $60,000, to millions of dollars for a wealthy man. The point to keep in mind is that the limits are quite flexible. Your broker will be willing to tell you what your credit limit is, and if you believe it prevents you from trading in the size you believe is appropriate for you, explain this to him. Mention any other relevant factors he might not be aware of, such as the fact that you will inherit a substantial amount of money, or that your wife just got a highly paid job, or that you got a major raise. Even without changes in your financial situation, if you are willing to come into the office and discuss the matter with the branch manager or whoever makes the credit determination, this could be favorable to you. The person you talk to will undoubtedly explain the risks of commodity trading and perhaps ask you to sign a legal document. But the very fact that someone other than your broker spoke to you about the risks of commodities, and that you acknowledged these risks, and that these facts have been recorded in your file makes it easier for the firm to increase your credit limit. If all else fails, you might try to get someone else, such as your father or brother, to guarantee your account for you.

CHAPTER 3
Basic Trading Strategies

A trading strategy is just a fancy word for a plan, but that doesn't make it any less essential. If there is one lesson this book teaches which is more important than any other, it is that you must have a strategy or plan. And by that we mean a strategy which covers the bad as well as the good.

The simplest plan is the one which most traders have in the back of their minds. It was first enunciated by that great philosopher Will Rogers, who said, "You buy a stock when it's going up, and after it has gone up, then you sell it." When he was asked what he would do if the stock did not go up after he bought it, he replied, "Then you don't buy it!" This illustrates the most common fault people make when getting into stock-index futures, namely to assume that just because they are long a contract it is likely to go up, or that just because they are short it will probably go down. Actually the odds are even that you will be wrong. Nevertheless, the temptation is great to assume that because we believe the market will go down (or up) it will probably do so. After all, unless we believe there are persuasive reasons why our opinion on the stock market is correct, we probably wouldn't be interested in stock-index futures in the first place.

Ask the average stock-index trader what his plan is and he will say something like, "The market is really overbought here, plus there are some basic negatives in the economy, so I'm going short four December contracts. My plan is to go short another four or six contracts when I have a good profit in the original four. Then I am not going to make the mistake so many people make. Remember, the bulls make money and the bears make money, but pigs never make money. So after I have a gain of about $4 in the second set of contracts, I am going to protect myself with stop-loss orders. Then as the market continues down, I will just keep lowering the price of my stop-loss orders. That way I don't have to worry about losing money and I will just keep making more and more money if the market goes down. If it really goes down far, I might go short some more contracts, but only on a conservative basis with stop-loss points close to the current price of the contracts."

WHAT IS A PLAN?

That is a plan? No, it definitely is not! I'll tell you why shortly. First, let me ask you whether this sounds in the least bit familiar: Maybe you think the market is going up, and so you have a similar "plan" on the upside. But I repeat, this is not a plan. Why isn't it? Because it is a dream. It is a wish list, an articulation of an emotional hope. In no way is it a plan! A plan must deal with the cold, harsh, hard, real world, which neither knows nor cares that you believe the market is about to move one way or another.

To make my point clear, let's diverge for a moment and talk about something which we are all familiar with, a weekend in the country. You decide it would be fun to take the family away to the beach for a weekend, and in the spirit of modern child psychology, you ask the kids to help plan what you should take along. You'll get no shortage of suggestions. Sis wants to bring her portable cassette deck with forty-seven of her favorite tapes, plus a beach towel and jogging outfit. John is bringing his baseball bat and glove, Frisbee, soccer ball and outfit, and kite, and Junior is all excited about bringing his new tricycle. That's what we expect from kids. But you and your spouse are the adults in charge. You have the responsibility of making sure the weekend goes smoothly under all circumstances. The kids don't have to worry about the things behind the scenes, but you have to make sure you have enough money, that the car's ready for the trip, that your accommodations are OK and so forth. But on a second, deeper level, you also have to think ahead, about what you'd do if things go wrong. What if it rains and you can't even go to the beach? Bring the Monopoly game and the slickers. What if someone gets hurt? Bring the first-aid kit. Headaches, upset stomachs? Bring the aspirin and the Alka-Seltzer. Extra blankets, suntan cream, insect repellent. These are the things you have to think of, and as a responsible, experienced parent, you do think of them. And because you thought ahead about what might go wrong, the weekend will be as much of a success as possible.

PREPARE FOR NEGATIVE MOVES

You can see that this simple illustration shows what I consider the quintessentially important aspect of planning—preparing ahead for what to do if things go wrong. Ask the kids to prepare for a weekend, and they think of beach balls. Great; we don't expect any more from them. But we do expect more from adults. And the same thing is true, only far more so, in a potentially very dangerous financial transaction such as taking a position in stock-index futures. If you have to plan ahead for the problems in a simple affair such as a family weekend, think of how much more important it is here! That is why the "plan" for stock-index trading we looked at before was no plan at all! Where in that plan did the trader take into consideration what he would do if the market went against him? Not until the very end, after he had presumably made money first on his original four contracts, and then on an additional four contracts. What is he going to do if he loses money from the beginning on his first four contracts? His "plan" does not even recognize this as a possibility. What if the market goes up suddenly after he has shorted an additional four contracts and is now short eight? Again his plan makes no mention of this. Therefore, this is no more a plan for successful stock-index trading program, than your kids wanting to bring a tricycle, baseball bat and tape cassettes is a "plan" for a family weekend at the beach.

A real plan must outline what you will do when you have losses at every stage. Otherwise it is not a meaningful plan. It is when things are going badly that we need a plan. No one needs a plan when he is making money. All he needs then is a Brink's truck to haul away his profits. And yet time after time, people begin to trade commodities and stock indexes without clearly and precisely determining what they are going to do if they start to lose.

Stock-index-futures trading takes risk. It is also a sum-zero activity, meaning that the total amount of money made in any period by the winners is equal to the amount lost by the losers. There is no way to be certain you will always win. In fact, due to the twin costs of commissions and of having to buy on the asked side and sell on the bid side, there is actually a net loss to traders as a whole when you combine the net winnings and the net losses for every day the market is open for business. Therefore, let us make it clear that this chapter and this book are not going to contain any magic formula that can make you money whether you are right or wrong on the direction of the market.

WHAT A PLAN CAN DO FOR YOU

Let me say once again: It is an absolute necessity to have a plan, and I believe that a plan can do at least two things for you: (1) It can enable you to control your risk and your losses to a very precise amount. (2) It can increase the probability of your making money when you are right. And these two factors are very significant; in fact, they are crucial. Without a plan your initial losses might be so great that you will be forced out of the market once and for all and then miss a tremendous move in your direction which would have made you a lot of money. Without a plan you might not be able to maximize your profits once the market does go in your favor, so that you would make a little money when the market moves in your favor and then give up much more than that when it goes in the other direction.

But the most important aspect of having a plan is that it puts you in command of the situation. You have thought out in advance what you will do under any circumstances. You made the plan when you were calm, could give adequate thought to all the various possibilities, and most important of all, were free from the strain and excitement that arise when you call up your broker and he tell you excitedly, "My God, look what's happening to your contract this morning! It's already down (or up) $2 and it's getting worse every trade. I think you should do something right now!" And, of course, you do. How much more professional to have thought out a plan in advance, and when your broker tells you this, you can simply note that you have already made your plans, that the orders are already in, and that you will call him at the end of the day to find out what was executed in accordance with your plan.

In planning your strategy in stock-index futures, the first and most important question is what to do when you suffer a setback. In fact, this is almost the only question. If your trades all make money, that's wonderful, and you don't need help from me. So let me show you right now why you absolutely must have a plan that can cover losses. Probably the largest group of people who don't think they need this kind of protection are those who buy some contracts and intend to hold onto them no matter what happens.

THE BUY-AND-HOLD PLAN

The thinking of this strategy is as follows. The trader decides that the market is near a low and is going to have a major rise, so he goes long a few contracts. Let's say the market is at 1,000 on the Dow Jones Industrial Average. The trader asks himself what is the worst thing that can happen to the market. Looking at the low of about 780 in August 1982, he thinks it reasonable to assume that if the market goes down it is not likely to go down very far below that point. Perhaps, to be quite safe, he will subtract another 50 points, bringing his projected low to 730. He thus makes the assumption that on a worst-case basis the market is not going to go below that point. He translates 730 on the DJIA into the approximate level on the index he is using and determines whether he can withstand a retreat down to that level. If he wants to use this strategy of buy and hold, he must be prepared to hold onto the contract even when it falls to this level, and not only must he want to do so, but he also must have the additional margin available so he *can* do so.

This seems like a pretty straightforward strategy. And it is, especially on the long side. But if you are going short because you believe the market is going down, then it becomes a bit harder to pick your absolute high. For so many years we have been having inflation, which has constantly eroded the value of the dollar, that it is not really safe simply to go back a few years and pick the high point on any average without factoring in inflation. And if you do factor in inflation, then you can be talking about some pretty large numbers. For example, if we use the Dow Jones Industrial Average again, it first reached 995 way back in January 1966. If you were to adjust this for the decline in the dollar since then, you would find that that figure expressed in today's dollars would be way above 2,000. And then it doesn't give any assurance that the Dow Jones wouldn't go above that point, because in addition to inflation, the economy has grown a great deal in real terms since 1966, so it would be quite reasonable to assume that in a major bull market stock prices would go substantially above their level in 1966, after correcting for inflation. So you would have to assume that in a major bull market the Dow Jones could go to 3,000. And, of course, if it ever did reach that figure, there is no guarantee that it would stop there.

Perils of Buying and Holding. What does a buy-and-hold approach mean in dollars and cents to someone who wants to use this strategy and is bullish on the market? Let's say that when you start, the Dow Jones is at 1,000, and this means that the index you want to use is at 135. Since the Dow Jones moves about 7 points to every one in the S&P 500 and the VLCA, we would figure that if the Dow Jones can fall from 1,000 to 730, for a loss of 270, we divide this by 7, meaning that our index could fall by almost 40 points. Since every point is worth $500, this means that we should be prepared to suffer a temporary loss of $20,000 per contract. In addition, when the market falls by that much, you can count on the fact that the contract you are long will go into a big discount from the index, probably by at least 3 points. Three times $500 adds on another $1,500, making an unrealized loss of $21,500 and an actual out-of-pocket expense of this much to cover the margin requirements.

But the real problem is that if the market goes down that far, it will be because there are very serious economic problems in the country, perhaps a major depression beyond the proportions of anything which has been seen since 1932. Given a case such as this, when the market does reach 730, what is to prevent it from going down farther? When the Dow Jones was at 1,000 and you thought it was actually going even higher than that, you also thought that 730 would be as low as it could get. Does that mean it isn't going to go any lower? Absolutely not. What usually happens is that by the time it gets near 730 you have become so discouraged and have lost so much money and are so concerned that the end is nowhere in sight that you close out your position. And can anyone blame you, after suffering a loss of over $20,000 on an investment of only $6,000? And knowing how much more you could lose? You see, once the market does get down to a level that low, all the pundits start predicting that it is now ready to go at least 100 points lower, and the extremists argue that it will go down another 200 points. And you are watching yourself lose about $500 more each day. It just doesn't make sense.

On the bearish side the case is even more extreme. Starting again with the Dow Jones at 1,000, you decide that the market is headed for a fall. You go short just one contract. The market heads into a bull market and climbs up to 2,000 with no end in sight. Dividing the rise of 1,000 on the Dow Jones by 7 means that your index will be up by approximately 143 without allowing for the fact that with a rise like that, all the futures would undoubtedly be selling at a substantial premium over the index price. With the market moving against you by 143 points, that means a loss to you of $500 times that, which comes to $71,500! And this could be just the beginning of your losses, because there is obviously no guarantee that a stock market which goes up 1,000 points is going to stop at precisely 2,000 on the Dow just because months earlier you had thought that this was as high as it was likely to go. So if you tried this sell-and-stay-short strategy on the bearish side you could be in the position of being out $71,500 on an initial investment of $6,000, with every likelihood that you would lose even more money in the future. But the real point is this: Which of us deciding to risk $6,000 would be able to sustain a loss of over ten times that amount? It just isn't feasible.

THE NEED TO LIMIT LOSSES

The clear conclusion of these two examples is that when you decide to speculate with stock-index futures, you are playing with dynamite. And how do the professionals work with dynamite? By taking every precaution they can. You *must*, not should, or ought to, or would be well advised to; but *must* limit your potential loss. You are speculating on something capable of enormous moves in either direction at any time. And you are there with something which has ten-to-one leverage! Not to limit your loss is inviting suicide! It is exactly like setting on an ocean journey across the Atlantic without a lifeboat or life preservers, on the theory that you really don't expect to run into storms or that the ship isn't likely to develop serious leaks; or to come back to our original example, just like setting out on a summer weekend without raincoats because it looks sunny to you right now. You just can't do it. When you go long or short even one stock-index-futures contract, you have a tiger by the tail, and you better make sure you can let go fast and get to safety.

You must have humility to be in stock-index futures. If you think you *know* what is going to happen in the stock market, then you are either going to be just plain lucky or you are going to be in for some rude surprises. And if you are lucky, your luck will last only so long before you too have the rude surprises. A good point to keep in mind when you put on any positions, long or short, is that today could be the beginning of the biggest move in the opposite direction that has ever been seen on Wall Street. And it is true. Neither you nor I nor anyone else can know what the stock market is going to do. And it is very possible that the very moment you select to go long a contract is the start of a major bear market. What are you going to do about it? Risk losing $21,500 on each contract? Or if you are going short, do you want to risk $71,500 on each contract? You won't and you can't and there is a simple method to prevent it all from happening.

WHY STOP-LOSS ORDERS ARE ESSENTIAL

The heart of any plan for trading stock-index futures must be stop-loss orders, for this is the better method of limiting your losses rationally. The only other rational method is to watch the market and close out your positions when they start moving against you, but this has two disadvantages. The first is that when the market starts moving against you, an emotional element becomes involved which makes it difficult to think rationally. You can do a far better job of deciding where your stop-loss orders should be if you take your time and do it at home with your charts, your calculator and other materials than when you are on a phone call to your broker. The second factor which makes this method simply not possible for most people is that there is no way they can be in constant touch with the market so they can decide to take action at just the right point. Please do not expect your broker to take on this responsibility. There is no way he can guarantee to do this, and even the most capable, well-meaning broker can get tied up in some other clients' affairs, be called away for an important meeting or just miss a level you asked him to watch for. Yes, he may be able to catch it four times in a row, for example, if you say, "Call me back if the contract moves more than 2 points against me." But the fifth time he may be in the cafeteria having his lunch when it happens, or you may not be reachable, and by the time the two of you get together the contract has moved 4 points or more against you. So for these two reasons just watching a contract and closing it out when you see it move by a certain amount against you is not a very good method of achieving the desired goal. And why fool around with such a sloppy method when there is such a precise, almost foolproof method available?

Good-Till-Canceled Orders. That method is the good-till-canceled stop-loss order (also called GTC or open order). Let's say you go long a futures contract at 144 and you don't want to risk more than 2 points. You would then enter a GTC stop order to sell your contract at 142. This means that if the contract trades at 142, your order is immediately activated and becomes an order to sell at the market. This does not mean you will sell your contract for 142, because in a rapidly falling market, once the contract trades at

142, the best bid on the floor may be 141.95 or 141.90 or whatever. But you will get the best price immediately available after your contract actually traded down to 142. The major problem with a stop-loss order is not that you will lose $0.05 or $0.10 in a rapidly falling market, but that there may be major news overnight and that the opening price of the contract may be substantially lower than your stop price. For example, assume the contract closes on Tuesday at 142.10, its low for the day. Your stop-loss order at 142 has not been activated. That night a major U.S. bank announces it has serious problems, and Wall Street starts to panic. Wednesday morning at 10:00 A.M. sharp Eastern Standard Time your contract opens at 140.30. What happens to your order? Since that was the first trade at or below 142, your stop-loss order now becomes a market order and will be sold for the best bid. That may be 140.30, or it may be quite a bit lower. Whatever the best bid at the time is, that is what you will get. It might be 2 whole points lower than your price for an unanticipated loss to you of $1,000 per contract, and of course if a real catastrophe had happened overnight, the contract could open 4 points lower or more.

The purpose of this example is to demonstrate that a stop-loss order is no guarantee that you will get out at the price you specify. There is no such guarantee at all, and not even an implication that you will. Rather, it is a market order triggered when the contract trades down to your limit. If you are short, then you would enter a stop-buy order, which would be triggered when the contract traded up to your limit. In either case, the risk is entirely yours as to the price at which the order actually will be executed.

Having pointed at the potential fallibility of a stop-loss order, let me state again that you must use one, because it is still the best method we have of containing losses. It is automatic in that no one has to watch the market constantly for you and when they see a certain level, rush to an order room and hope that the order clerk can process the order right away and that when it gets to the exchange floor someone will take it right out to the pit. No, at the very second the contract trades at your predetermined level, that becomes a market order on the floor of the exchange. There can be no slipup. The other advantage is that it is certain. No matter how fast the market is falling, you will be out. These are two extremely important points, and in fact are the determining points of why you want to use stop-loss orders.

Stop-Limit Orders. There is a variation on the stop-loss order which can prevent you from suffering the larger-than-anticipated losses we discussed earlier in case the market gaps open down 2 points. This is a stop-limit order. You state that you want to sell your contract when it gets to 142 and that you will not sell it unless you can get a limit, which you might set at 141.80. This means that if the market opens with a trade at 141, your order would be activated because the contract traded below 142, but it would not be filled because they could not sell it at 141.80. Your order would then remain as an order to sell at 141.80, and if the contract goes back up that high, you would then sell it for that. The negatives are that if the contract does not go up to 141.80, you will not sell the contract. Therefore, when you probably want to sell it the most—that is, when things look worst and the market is falling the fastest—you will not be able to get out of the contract. So while a stop-limit order sounds great when you first hear about it, it really doesn't do the job. Better to get out with a lower price than you wanted than not to get out at all.

Being Whipsawed. Let's look at another major disadvantage of the stop-loss order, and this is that you can get stopped out by a random sudden drop which is over in an instant, leaving you high and dry and having sold out at the low of the day. For example, you may buy a contract for 135 and decide that you will protect yourself by entering a stop-loss at 132. The contract falls and is trading at 132.50. Suddenly, without any warning, a flood of sell orders hits the floor, and without any fall in the underlying index, your contract drops down, just touches 132 for a moment, thus triggering your order, which goes off at 132, and within seconds the contract begins to climb again and is shortly back to 132.50. So you have sold at what turns out to be the low for the day, and you are out of your position although you really wanted to be in it at 132.50. The next day the contract could continue on its way up, and you have been stopped out by a freakish drop.

This is what we call being whipsawed. The skeptics to whom this happens will always say that the floor traders were aware of their stop-loss order and deliberately took the price of the futures contract down to their level so that the floor traders could pick up their contract at 132. Rest assured that if your stop-loss order was for just one contract, it would not pay for anyone to do all the selling necessary to get a contract to move down $0.50 to pick up your one contract. If you have a stop-loss order for twenty contracts and you are trading in a thinly traded contract, such as one nine months out, then such a scenario may be possible, but even then there are usually too many other people around who would be buying the contract to permit someone to bring the price down just to snap up your single contract.

Let's get back to the problem here, which is that the use of the stop-loss order here did not have the result you wanted. You wanted to get out at 132 because you were afraid if it got down that low it would very likely continue down farther, and you had lost enough money at 132 so you didn't want to risk more. Therefore you put in your stop-loss order at that point, perhaps thinking that if it went down much farther you would buy back in at a lower price. Instead you got sold out and the contract went right back up, and you realize that you would have been much better off if you had never entered the stop-loss order. Now you are faced with the unpleasant dilemma of either being out of what might be a very bullish market when you want to be in it, or of buying in at a higher price and losing profits which should have been yours.

But that is the way it is. In this case the stop-loss order did not do for you what you wanted it to do. But nothing can be done about that. And if you analyze what happened, you could conclude that the fault was not with the stop-loss order but with the market, over which we have no control. The stop-loss order was supposed to get you out at 132, because you decided that if the contract went that low you wanted no part of it. It did, and you got out. So the stop-loss order kept its part of the bargain. Your complaint, therefore, should not be addressed to the stop-loss order, but to the market, which did exactly the opposite of what you wanted it to do. You expected that once the market touched 132 it would continue to go down. Unfortunately for you, you were wrong. But we are often wrong about the market. That's nothing new. What is new here, at least for you, is that you got sandbagged.

My purpose is simply to point out that a whipsaw can indeed happen and that nothing can be done about it. The advantages of using stop-loss orders still far outweigh the disadvantages. The only disadvantage here is that you might miss out on part of the future profit. But in other cases if you did not use a stop-loss order, the cost to you could be many, many thousands of dollars. In this respect it is a bit like using a seat belt in your car. Statistics show that seat belts would save thousands of lives a year if they were used at all times by

American drivers and passengers. Yet it is nevertheless true that in a small percentage of accidents, a person who is killed or seriously injured would not have been if he were not wearing a seat belt. This is tragic and ironic, but it does not change the basic conclusion that you should wear seat belts because you have a much better chance of reaching your destination alive than if you don't.

Sure, stop-loss orders are not perfect. You might almost say that their use is the worst possible method to get out of the market, because you will frequently be selling out at the low, or buying in at the high, just the opposite of what you should be doing to make money. I am reminded of Winston Churchill's comment on democracy. He said that democracy had to be the worst form of government. (Can you imagine people actually deciding who they want to rule themselves? Do the inmates elect the head of the asylum?) Then Churchill continued by saying that democracy was indeed the worst form of government, except that it was better than every other form which had ever been tried.

So indeed a stop-loss order is a terrible way to limit a loss. The only trouble is that it is better than any other means ever devised. Now let's consider ways by which we can make them less terrible.

OVERCOMING THE DISADVANTAGES: STAGGERED STOPS

First is the problem discussed above of a sudden drop which touches off the order, after which the market climbs merrily out of sight. This problem can be virtually eliminated if you are trading more than one contract by placing your stop-loss orders at varied limits. For example, if you are trading four contracts, instead of placing a stop-loss order to sell all four if the contract drops to 155, you could place one order to sell at 157, one at 156 and so forth. In this way if the contract just touches 157 and then goes back up you have only sold one contract, so your position still is 75% intact. If it goes down to 156 and then swoops back up, you still have half of your position. And if it touches 155 and then goes back up you have only one contract left, but you sold one two points higher and one one point higher, so at least you have an extra $1,500 that you wouldn't have had if you had simply put in a stop at 155 for all four. With this extra money you can have more confidence to go back into the market and put on some long positions again. Just how you vary the stops is up to you, but consider having them spaced farther apart. For instance, if you are trading three contracts and are thinking of a stop-loss order at 155, perhaps the best strategy for you is to place one at 157, one at 155 and one at 153. Incidentally, some traders believe it is not a good idea to use whole numbers like this, because they incur psychological resistance. Therefore, if they were using a stop-loss order they would place it at 156.80, etc., so that if the contract went down to 157 and then touched off a lot of buy orders and didn't go any farther, their order would not go off. Similarly, if you are short, you might consider placing your stop-buy orders at 157.20.

Keep Close to the Market Price. The second technique which can make stop-loss orders more effective is placing them closer to the current market. Let's say you go short a contract at 145. If your biggest worry is that you will get stopped out before the great market crash occurs (which you *know* is going to come soon), then you will probably want to make sure that your stop is far away so it won't get triggered by a little rise. Therefore you will place the limit at 150 to give yourself plenty of room. The problem is that by the time your order goes off at 150 you have lost $2,500 per contract. This is such a large amount that you probably are very discouraged at that point and don't really have any strategy to recoup your losses and make a profit. By placing your stop-loss order closer to your entry price you may be forced out sooner, but what is the risk? If the market does an about-face as soon as your order is executed, you can always come back in. True, it will be at a lower price, but if as you believe, this could be the beginning of a major bear market, then missing out on a few cents or even a few dollars will not be tragic. On the other hand, if the market advances by 5 points before you get out, then your flexibility—and self-esteem—are reduced.

Let's take another example showing the value of using stops close to where the market is. This is the actual case of a man who made a substantial amount of money being long a total of ten contracts, which he had accumulated at various prices. He was trading the S&P 500, which had risen to 124. He had been using stop-loss orders to protect himself, and many of them had been triggered off. But it happened to be in a period of a major market advance, and after a few weeks he realized that every time part of his position was sold out on a stop-loss order, he eventually bought it back at a higher price. His conclusion was to stop using stops at a price likely to be reached by normal day-to-day declines in the market and place his stops at a point far enough away from the current contract price so he would only get stopped out when there was a major market reversal. He placed his stops at 114, a full 10 points below the market. Just at the time he entered that stop-loss order, the market began a sharp downturn, and he stayed with his positions until he was stopped at 114. The problem was that although he had a very good profit at 124, his average purchase price was 118. This is because he had started in with one contract at 110, then added another when it went up 2 points, then added two more contracts when they went up some more, and so forth. He had been long all ten contracts only for the last few points of the rally. On the way down, however, he was long the full ten contracts for the entire 10-point fall. Therefore, by the time he was stopped out he had seen his very good profit become transformed into a sizable loss. And he was distraught. Here was the market, 4 points higher than when he had come into it, he had been bullish all the way, and yet he was now out a substantial amount of money and wasn't even in the market anymore, so that if it did start going up again he would have to get in at a higher price. It just didn't seem fair.

Well, we're sorry, but as John F. Kennedy said a number of years ago, "Life isn't fair." It may not be fair, but it still is capable of analysis, at least in this small aspect of making money in stock-index futures. The obvious point from the above example is that if you place your stop-loss points so far away that you only get shut out in a major move against you, it may almost be too late when you get out. The purpose of a stop-loss order, whenever possible, is not to get out with a large loss just before you have to declare bankruptcy, but rather to get out when you still have a good profit.

The man in our example should have been aware that although he was playing with ten contracts, he really had only made meaningful money in a few of them. Therefore, since the purpose of a stop-loss order is to protect your profits whenever possible, he should have placed his stop-loss orders at a higher level. The appropriate step for him would have been to place a stop-loss order for perhaps five contracts at a point just a few points below the market, since he had only a relatively small profit in the last five contracts he had acquired. If the market went down to that point, he could have placed his remaining stops at substantially lower points, because now he was only losing half as much as before on every point down. By getting out early with his five contracts, he would protect his profits in those and could then afford to ride a lower market.

STOP-LOSS ORDER SUMMARY

The basic purpose of stop-loss orders is to make sure you keep what profits you have, and if you don't have any, that you lose as little as possible. Think of it this way. If you don't get out, you can possibly lose a very substantial amount of money. On the other hand, if you do get out and the market then turns around, the worst thing that can happen to you is that you will miss out on a possible profit. Balance these two worst-case possibilities. Which would you rather not have happen to you? Lose a substantial amount of money, or not make a possible profit? Most of us would rather not lose the money. Once money is gone it may never be possible to replace it. A missed profit can be earned back in a hundred different ways over the coming years.

After looking at these alternatives, most people will agree that "discretion is the greater part of valor," which in more down-to-earth terms is expressed, "He who fights and runs away lives to fight another day." There are no heroes in the commodities boardrooms; no Congressional Medals of Honor are awarded to those who stick with their positions in the face of an unfavorable market. On the contrary, their absences in the next few days will scarcely be noticed. But the person who ducked out when things started going against him could be the star attraction next week when he takes on his positions in a favorable market.

This has been a full discussion of stop-loss orders, but it was worth it because they are the kingpin of any stock-index strategy. The basic point of the strategy is to have a plan, and the *sine qua non* of the plan is to know precisely what you are going to do when the market goes against you. There are only three things you can do. One is to add more positions, which greatly increases your exposure and your margin costs and may therefore be out of the question for many people. The second is to do nothing, which as we saw could lead to a ruinous loss and drain of funds to cover margin requirements. The third and frequently most sensible course of action is to get out while you still can. The best method of doing this is the stop-loss order. Since it is really the key to the entire program of making money, it is important to understand it thoroughly.

To summarize our discussions about stop-loss orders, we have drawn the following conclusions. (1) Always use a stop-loss order at some level on every one of your positions, unless you are willing to suffer losses of up to $21,500 or more on the long side and $71,500 on the short side. (2) When you are trading more than one contract, use different stop-loss points for different contracts. For example, if you are trading twelve contracts, you might have stop-loss orders at four different points for three contracts each. The advantage is that if the market just dips a little against you, you still will have 75% of your position. But if it takes a big drop, you will have sold out a significant part of your position at a price above the current price and therefore will be in pretty good shape to decide to go back into the market another day. (3) Place your initial stop-order points close to the current market price. The only drawback in having your stop-loss orders close to current price is that you will pay some extra commissions (which are small in comparison to the sums at risk) and that you might miss out on some profits.

TAKING THE INITIAL POSITION

Now that we've discussed the most important part of the plan—what to do when the market goes against you—we can get into the second most important part. This is what comes first chronologically and what you may believe is the most important part, namely whether you should go long or short, at what price you should get into the market and with how many positions. The first question is whether you want to go long or short. The answer depends upon many factors, but the final determinants are your personal views. And your conclusions are the distillation of every bit of information you have received over the past few years, from old sayings you may remember from your youth, to what you heard on the radio this morning as you were driving to the office. Whatever conclusion you come to will probably be well reasoned, but that does not mean it is very likely to be correct. It is a cold statistical fact that for every person who goes long a stock-index future, someone else goes short. Both believe they are doing the right thing. Therefore, whether the market goes up or down, half of the traders will be wrong. So perhaps the best advice I can give here is that it is important to have humility when you decide. Most stock-index traders rely on their views of the stock market derived from general information to guide them as to whether they should go long or short. But there are other strategies which deserve your consideration.

FOLLOWING THE TREND

First is to follow the trend. You may be bearish, but nevertheless if the market is going up, it is easier to imagine the upward trend continuing than to imagine it will turn around and start to move in your direction. Therefore, you might wish to go long and be protected by close stop-loss orders in case the major turn you are expecting does occur. But if the trend continues, you can get in and out quickly with a neat profit. And you can do so on a move that wouldn't even cover the transaction costs of a stock trader.

Therefore, if you see that the market is moving up, one reasonable approach is to go long. You protect yourself with a stop-loss order and wait to see what happens. If the trend continues, all is well and good. You could raise your stop-loss limit and see what happens again. If the trend keeps on, you can just keep on raising your stop-loss order until finally your position is closed out with a good profit for you. The point here is that with stock-index futures it is possible to play a short-term trend for a profit even if you believe it is not a major direction of the stock market.

Trading Against the Spread. A second strategy to help you decide whether to go long or short is to trade against the spread. By this I mean that if the consensus view is that the market is going to go up, you go short. If the consensus is that the market is going to go down, you go long. How do you tell what the consensus is? That is the simplest question in this book. The futures contracts will tell you by their prices. If the prices of the futures are substantially above the price of the underlying index, then they are telling you that more speculators want to go long the futures contract than want to go short. The higher the premium over the current index, the greater the degree of conviction held by the futures speculators. When the futures on the S&P 500 and the VLCA are 3 or more points above the index, there is a good amount of optimism in the air, and when they are that much below the index, traders are pessimistic. But generally they will not be that far apart from the index.

Typically, if the market has a good day and the indexes rise by 2 points, you may see the futures go up by about 3 points. Perhaps the next day the rally continues up another 2 points, and again the futures may go up by 3 points. This means that at the end of the second day, the futures are 2 points higher above the index than they were in the beginning. Now, granted we don't know what is going to happen on the third day. But if it does continue to go up another 2 points, the future is probably not going to continue to outpace it, because it already has the additional 2-point cushion built up. Rather it would probably advance just the 2 points. But if the market doesn't do anything, it is almost certain that the futures are going to go down. That 2-point premium is the result of two straight days of upward motion, which encouraged all the bulls to add to their positions and scared the bears into covering their positions, which means that they were also buyers. So naturally the futures rose 2 points beyond where they were in relation to the index. But now let the market pause, and the bears will begin to sell again, and some of the bulls will decide that this small rally has reached its peak and they will begin to take profits, which means that they too will be sellers. Therefore, if the index does nothing, it is extremely likely that the futures will fall by perhaps a point.

The third possibility is that the index falls, and in this case we have the above scenario played out again, but with even greater intensity. Now the bears are beginning to make money, and they are encouraged to short more positions, meaning that there is increased selling. Now the bulls are taking profits and are also getting concerned that not only might it be the end of a chance to make any further profits, but also that if they don't get out fast they will begin to see their profits turn into losses. So they become sellers in a much bigger way. And as the futures start to go down, more and more bulls and bears will be sellers.

What this means for you is that the odds are in your favor if you short a futures contract substantially above the index, particularly if the premium has been built up in just the past few days. Similarly, when the futures are selling at a discount, the odds are in your favor to buy the futures contract. As we have just seen, there are only three possibilities for tomorrow: The index will go up, stay about where it is or go down. You could be a winner in two out of three. Those aren't bad odds. And on a slightly deeper level, this can also be good strategy.

So far we have looked just at the mathematics of the futures against the index. But if you consider the psychology of speculators and investors, there is strong evidence to support the contention that when almost everyone expects the market to go down, it will go up; and that when almost everyone expects it to go up, it will go down. This is the theory of the contrarians. Therefore, the premium or discount the futures have to their indexes can also be a valuable insight into the psychology of the marketplace. And since the consensus is always wrong according to this theory, you have another reason for being more likely right when you go against the prevailing view of the market as revealed through the futures price. Not only are the odds on your side from a purely random viewpoint, but also there is probably a pretty good chance that you will be right on which way the actual index moves.

Selecting the Entry Price. Once you have made the major decision of whether to go long or short, the next decision is at what price to enter the market. This really depends upon your reason for being in the market. If you believe it is about to start a big move down or up, you should get in by placing market orders. If you are in for a short-term trend about which you don't have very strong convictions, you might want to get in at a price below the current price. The way to do this is to determine what a likely low is based upon normal intraday trends, then place a limit-buy order on a good-till-canceled basis. For example, if the low yesterday for your futures contract was 143.70 and it closed at 144.50 and opens this morning at the same price, you might not be in any hurry to buy at that price. Instead, you could assume it very likely that with normal fluctuations in the price it is likely to get within a few points of its low yesterday. Therefore you enter an order to buy a contract at 143.90, just $0.20 above yesterday's low. If the contract is available at that price, you will automatically buy it. So you enter the order, and if it is filled, fine. If not, you haven't lost much, since you didn't have very strong convictions in the first place. If the next day the market is up, you can increase your limit for the next day if you choose.

Entering with a Stop-Loss Order. The third way of getting into the market is used the least, and that is to put in a stop-loss order to buy when the price rises to a certain point, or sell when it goes below a certain point. You would use this method if you were trying to follow the first rule mentioned in this chapter and wanted to follow the trend but weren't sure that there was any trend right now. For example, your index could be at 83, and it has been trading around there for about four days. You believe that a breakout could easily occur on the downside, and if it does, you want to be short that contract. Instead of giving your broker a headache by calling him every twenty minutes to find out what's happening, you can simply decide in advance that if the contract ever trades below 81, this will be a clear sign that the new breakout is under way, and you want to be in on it. Therefore you place a GTC stop order to sell a contract at 80.90. If it gets down there, fine, you are in. And if it never gets down that low, you won't be in, but then you haven't missed much, either. If you are wondering at what level to place your stop orders, look at a chart of the contract you are considering trading. If you want to go short and are looking for a major breakout, then you would look at how low the contract has gotten in the previous few weeks. You would then conclude that if it gets below the lowest point it has reached in the past few weeks, this means a new breakout on the downside, and it is the time to short.

The reasoning behind this is that if it has gotten to a certain low point before, let's say 145, and not gotten below that point, then there are a lot of longs who will have losses once it gets below this point and they will be running to get out, perhaps automatically with stop-loss orders, which will send the market down even farther. On the other hand, there will be a number of shorts who will not have profits until it gets below that level, but once it does, then all those who have shorted within the past few weeks will have a profit. Following the old maxim "Cut your losses short and let your profits ride," they will not be buying contracts but will be sticking with their positions. In fact, many of them will be increasing their positions as the contract goes down, so they also will be additional sellers. Thus, this theory holds, once a contract falls below one of its old support levels, there is likely to be increased selling from both the longs and the shorts, and this will just further increase the downward pressure on the price. Therefore, the strategy evolves of placing a stop order below the past lows and selling the contract when it breaches these lows.

This strategy can work just as well on the upside. Let's say that you are bullish on the market but don't know exactly when to get in. You have decided that you don't want to trade small moves but are looking for a major trend to ride. The contract you are looking at is 137 right now. You consult a recent chart and discover that its recent highs have been 139, 140.5 and 138. Following this chain of reasoning, you conclude that if the contract ever gets above 141, all those who are long the contract will have profits, and they will be inclined to hold onto their contracts and even to buy more, while all those who are short will have losses and will be inclined to reduce their exposure by buying in contracts, all of which will result in further moves upward on the contract. Accordingly you enter your order to buy a contract at 141 stop with a good-till-canceled order.

DETERMINING THE NUMBER OF CONTRACTS

Now that we've discussed how to decide whether your first position should be long or short and how you determine at what price level to enter, the only other question is how many contracts you will start with. The basic rule has to be to start small. It would be quite unusual indeed if the stock market were experiencing one of its very few "once-in-a-lifetime" opportunities to get in on the beginning of a major new trend the very day you decide to start trading stock-index futures. Rather, the almost certain situation will be that the market is about to do what it invariably does: In the words of J. P. Morgan, "It will fluctuate." And if you miss the chance to make a big hit on your first trade, you will undoubtedly have plenty of opportunities in the future. If, however, you go in with a large number of contracts on your first trade and lose a large amount of money, you may never have a chance to make it back. Therefore, the way to get started in stock-index futures is to start small. For many people, even one contract of the S&P 500 or the VLCA is a substantial commitment. Remember, they frequently move by 3 points in a day, which is $1,500. If you're on the wrong side, this means you can lose $1,500 within twenty-four hours of starting out. How does that make you feel? Anxious to increase your potential loss by going in for a larger number of contracts? If you want to start out really small, begin with the NYSE, because it generally moves only half as much as the others, since the average on which it is based is about half as large as the others.

Starting small doesn't mean you have to stay small. If you like what's happening, you can easily increase the number of contracts you are trading. But if you start large, and the market goes against you, then the only way you can decrease your exposure is by realizing your paper losses. And who wants to do that?

ALTERNATIVE TRADING STRATEGIES

Once you have taken your original position, you are in the position of having to plan out your trading strategies. As we have mentioned, the foundation of most trading strategies is the stop-loss order, which acts like a parachute. When your plane gets into trouble, you jump through the doorway and float gently to earth. Let the heroes go down with the plane. Therefore I recommend that as soon as your broker reports what price you got on your initial position, give him a good-till-canceled stop order to get out of the position when it goes against you to the point you have selected.

Buy and Hold. A stop-loss order is not the only way you can handle a market move against you. You might have the resources and the outlook to be one of the buy-and-hold people we discussed earlier. In this case, you simply stick to your position, convinced that you will turn out to be correct before the expiration date. But please do not adopt this strategy without considering the large potential losses you can have and the enormous margin requirements when the market moves that far against you. If you can't absorb either the potential losses or the margin requirements, you cannot accept the buy-and-hold strategy. You will have to use a modification of it, which is to place a stop-loss order at a point a long distance from the market so it is not too likely ever to be executed. But at least it will be there in an emergency.

Averaging Up or Down. The third method of dealing with a loss on your initial position is to average down. This means that as the price moves against you, you buy or sell additional contracts at continually better prices. For example, if you are expecting a market decline and short a future at 137, and the next day it is 139, and the next 141, you could then short another contract at 141. This would be called averaging up, because the average sale price of your contracts goes up to the average of 137 and 141, which is 139, or 2 points higher than your original sale price. This is advantageous for you, and the method works just as well when you are long and the market price is falling. The advantage of this method over a stop-loss order is that you are doing something positive about adverse market conditions. You are making them work for you by improving your average price, rather than against you, as in a stop-loss order when you are realizing a loss and getting out of the market at a worse price. In theory, then, a very strong argument can be made for averaging up or down rather than using a stop-loss order. Obviously it can be used only when you have started out small and have plenty of margin available. Once you average down or up, you now have twice the loss potential you had before. So, not only do you have the loss from your original position, even though it is only an unrealized loss, but you also have the potential of losing twice as much as before.

Then if the market goes against you some more, you are losing twice as much money for each point in the contract price. To be consistent, if the market moves against you again, you would then buy or sell another contract at the new price. This can be continued until the market turns around.

It must be pointed out that our previous discussion about the difficulties of the buy-and-hold strategy apply here, but in spades. In that type of strategy you are losing money only on your original position, but here you could be losing money on a constantly expanding position, which means that as long as the market moves against you, you are snowballing your losses. For most people it would be very hard to sustain this strategy very long. Another problem is that as you increase your sales (or purchases), their effect upon your average price becomes less and less pronounced. When you had just one position, adding another one moved your average price to the midpoint between the two prices. But when you have two positions and you add another position, the existing positions outweigh the new position by two to one, so your average price moves down only by a third. If you ever got to the situation where you have five contracts and are adding another, the price of your average contract would move only a sixth of the distance between the previous average price and the price of your new contract. Thus, as the positions move against you, and as you lose more and more money, the benefit of averaging down becomes less and less effective. If you wanted to keep on improving your average price, you would actually have to double the number of positions each time. That means that if you started out with one contract and then bought or sold another one, the next time you took on a new position you would have to use two contracts, the next time it would have to be four and so forth. Clearly it would not be too long before you would be at the limit of your resources.

Short-Term Moves. One modification of the averaging-down or averaging-up strategy is to decide in advance that you will do this for a relatively short market move, but that if the move turns out to be a major trend, then you will close out your positions and take your loss as gracefully as possible. For example, if you are bullish on the market and you go long a contract at 90 and the market goes down, you might then buy another contract at 86, and another at 82. This gives you the benefit of reducing your average price to 86. You now have three contracts, which means that if the market keeps going down, you are losing three times as much money per point as originally. Thus you place a stop-loss order to close out your position at some point significantly lower down. You might enter stop-loss orders to sell one contract at 78, one at 76 and one at 74. The thinking behind this is that as long as the market is simply moving within a narrow range, as it usually does, you will take advantage of the averaging-down technique to lower your effective purchase cost. But when it becomes apparent that the decline is not just a normal market correction of the type that happens every week but rather a major market move of the type that only occurs a few times a year, then it is time to get out.

WHAT TO DO WHEN YOU'RE MAKING MONEY

So far this chapter has been rather gloomy. That was quite intentional, so you would not be under the false impression that it was easy to make money in stock-index futures. It is not. But as we said in the beginning, it is a bit easier to make money when you have a good handle on how you will control your losses. Fortunately, real life does occasionally have its pleasant surprises. Yes, there are times when you will put on a position, and miracle of miracles, the market will move with you! You will actually have a profit at the end of the first day! Lest you think, however, that you have now discovered the secret to unlimited riches, let me state that in my opinion it is much better for you in the long run to lose on your first trade than it is to win at it. The reason is very simply that when you lose on your first trade, you develop respect for the dangers of the market. When you make money initially it is easy to become overconfident and start to lose sight of the potentially overpowering dangers lurking around every turn. It is the person who makes money on his first trade who often ends up the biggest loser on his last.

In this respect I am reminded of a former client of mine who decided to speculate on gold futures in October 1979. He went long one contract of October 1980 gold at a price of 457. As many of you may recall, the price of gold began to go up, and it just kept on going up and up. His contract reached $500 an ounce, then $600, then $700 and then $800. I remember reviewing his commodity account one day and saying to myself in amazement, "This guy has made almost $50,000 in just a little over three months on an investment of just $4,000." Needless to say, the client was delighted, but he decided not to sell out because he was convinced gold would go much higher.

Then it went on up to $850 and he called me and said that if his contract ever went over $900 an ounce it was a sign that there was a breakout and it was going to go much higher. By then there was almost a buying panic, and gold futures were going up the limit every day, which meant that it was impossible to buy them because they would jump up the limit in the first three minutes and then not trade for the rest of the day. A few days later he called me again and said, "Max, it probably won't be possible to buy any contracts today, but put in the order just below the limit and we may get lucky." Sure enough, we were able to buy one at 946. Two days later he asked me to see if I could buy him another one, and I did at the same price. He now had three contracts.

Within a few days the price of gold began to fall rapidly. He was asked to send in a substantial amount of margin, which he did. Finally when the price of his contract fell to $700 he just couldn't meet the margin call, and he sold out. The final result? His profit of over $50,000 had been converted into a loss of over $25,000 in just a few weeks, because he let his initial profit blind him to the continuous dangers always present in every commodities market, which includes the stock-index futures. Never forget the old Wall Street saying that it is easier to make profits than to keep them.

In this section, we are going to learn how to trade when you have profits. There are three possibilities: pyramiding, holding and hoping, and raising stop-loss levels.

Pyramiding. Let's start with the simplest example. You go long a contract at 140. The contract price moves up in the next few weeks to 152. Your profit of 12 points is $6,000. You now have three basic choices. First, you can sell out your position and take that profit and go home. But this is hard to do, especially if it seems that the market will continue up. Second, you can hold your position, and make a selling decision at a later date. Or third, you can decide that since it was so much fun to make money with one contract, it should be twice as much fun to make money with two contracts. And isn't there that famous saying, "Cut your losses short, and let your winnings ride"? What better way to let your winnings ride than to double the number of contracts? And the commodity margin rules make it so easy. If your initial margin requirement was $6,000 then you have already made enough profit to cover the entire margin requirement on the second contract. So your friendly broker may suggest that you buy another contract, because you won't even have to send in any money, and then instead of just making $6,000 on a 12-point rise in the contract you could really make some important money—for example, $12,000.

The real advantage of this strategy is that once you have doubled your position to two contracts, it becomes even easier to go to three contracts, because now your contract only has to move up 6 points to earn you the additional $6,000 you need for the margin on another contract. And then if you go to three contracts, it only takes a rise of 4 points to make you an additional $6,000. And with four contracts, the price only has to go up 3 points. By this time you really ought to be feeling rich. You have put up only $6,000, yet the four contracts you are trading have margin requirements of $24,000. What is really exciting is that now every time the index goes up by just a point, you will be making $2,000. If it moves up another 12 points, as it did originally, then instead of having a profit of just $6,000, you will have a profit of $24,000. Now, that's something to be proud of!

Pitfalls of Pyramiding. This strategy of increasing your positions as they go in your favor is called pyramiding, and the only trouble with it is that almost inevitably you will lose almost all your money doing it. I can explain very easily, and the explanation requires only two assumptions. The first is that no market moves in the same direction forever. Therefore the market will eventually stop moving in the direction which is making you richer. Then it will begin to move in the other direction. All the profit you made with one or two contracts can disappear very quickly when you have four or eight or whatever number of contracts. The second assumption is that no one blows a whistle when the market reaches its top, which means that you will probably not be aware that a top has been reached nor realize that the market is changing direction and taking your profits along with it.

Let me illustrate with the example we started. Our trader got into the market with one contract at 140. By adding positions as soon as his profits had generated enough money to cover the initial margin requirements of additional contracts, he had four contracts with the market at 162. This means that our trader has just experienced an advance of 22 points, which is a tremendous advance by any standards. But he probably doesn't think so, and he is waiting for the real rally to get under way, during which he will be making his $2,000 a point rather than a puny $500.

So if it took him 22 points to make all this profit and increase his positions, how many points on the downside will it take for him to lose all his profit? No, not 22 points. A mere 5.5 points—not much of a market correction after a 22-point advance. That could happen in just two days, and the way reactions to sustained moves occur, it very likely wouldn't take any more than one day to wipe out all his profits, or even to put him in a loss situation.

Obviously, if our trader had been even luckier, the example would be more extreme. At 162 with four contracts, another three points to 165 would enable him to add a fifth contract, and then it would take only a little more than a 2-point rise to add another contract. So at 167 he could have six contracts. Now every point down would cost him $3,000, so it would take only a decline to 157 to wipe out all his profit. And this seems like such a little decline, considering that he got in at 140. In other words, it took a rise of 26 points to have such a large profit that one could go to six contracts, and it took a decline of only 10 points to wipe out that entire profit. It may not seem fair, but that's the way it is.

Conclusion: If you are going to pyramid your winnings, it is more important than ever to protect your profit with stop-loss orders. Remember that you have just loaded the deck against yourself. What took perhaps 24 points to create can be disintegrated in just 10 points. And you will be saying to yourself, "I just don't believe that I lost the whole profit." And of course what is even worse is that it only takes a few more points before your former terrific profit is actually transformed into a major loss, yet the market may be 15 points higher than when you got into it. If you really want to take on added risks in the hope of making larger profits, that is your business. But remember that you must protect yourself even more carefully than when you had fewer contracts. Use your stop-loss positions, and bring them in closer than you had them before. Perhaps the best method is to use staggered stop-loss positions and place the highest stop-loss points at the prices you paid for the latest positions. In that way the loss can be contained, and in fact you are treating your latest positions as short-term trading contracts, which you will sell out quickly if things go against you.

Holding and Hoping. Now let's examine the second possibility of behavior when you find yourself with a profitable position. Let's say you bought three contracts and the market has gone in your favor, perhaps up 4 points, giving you a profit of $6,000. You have read the previous paragraphs and decide that pyramiding is not for you, so you are not going to add to your four contracts. What should you do? The first possibility is to do nothing at the present time and hope that the contract continues to go higher, with the idea in the back of your mind that you will sell out when it does. I strongly recommend against this course because there is the constant danger that the market will move against you and your entire profit will be wiped out. This course of conduct (it would be too kind to call it a course of "action") is what we might call the wishful-thinking syndrome. It works about as well as wishing very hard that the good fairy will leave a $1,000 bill under your pillow tonight. Futures are a tough, cruel world, and you must be prepared. You must take some form of action if you don't want to be totally at the mercy of the market. There are two types of action you can take.

The first and simplest is to put in a market order right now to sell your positions and take your profit. This has the obvious advantage of taking you out of the market and hence eliminating all your risk and at the same time giving you a good profit. Naturally, if you have reason to believe the market is going to go down, this is what you are going to do. But usually we don't have such clear visions of the future. In these cases taking a profit means limiting your profit, which we never like to do.

A more positive possibility is to put in a limit order at a price above the present price. For example, your contract is now at 168, and rather than selling now you place a good-till-canceled order to sell at 171 because you believe there is a good chance it might reach that level in the next few days. Having an order like that is a much better way of getting out than just calling up your broker from time to time and seeing where the contract is and selling at whatever price it happens to be when you are talking to him. With an order in, the contract might just suddenly pop up for only two minutes, and your order could go off at almost the high for the day. This type of order works particularly well in short-term trading, when you place the sell order at what appears to be a reasonable trading range for the day.

The advantage of placing a limit order like this is that if it goes off, you have made yourself a nice little profit and are free to decide whether you want to go short, go long or just stay on the sidelines for a while. The disadvantage is that since you are now out of the market, you will miss out if the move in your favor turns out to be just the beginning of a major market advance. Thus we say that this strategy is perfect for short-term trading but not good for anyone who wants to capture the large moves. In short, it violates the old maxim of cutting your losses short but letting your winnings ride.

Raising Stop-Loss Levels. The third possibility of what you can do when the market goes in your favor is to move your stop-loss levels with the market, so that as the market moves in your favor you are constantly locking in a part of your gains. For example, if you go long a contract at 168 and it moves up to 171, for a move up of 3 points, you could increase your stop-loss order by those 3 points. If you originally placed your stop-loss order at 166, then you would move it up to 169, thus locking in a profit of a point. If the market continued to move up, you would just keep on increasing your stop-loss levels. The advantage of this is that you do not have to decide when to sell your contract. As far as you are concerned, if the market keeps on going up, you will never sell the contract. Thus you are letting your winnings ride until a market correction comes along. In effect, you are not predetermining when to sell your contract but rather letting the market decide for you. You are saying, "I have no idea how much higher the market is going to go. Why should I sell out when the market is going up? Rather I will let the market decide for me when to sell out. When the market has stopped going up and begins to come down, that is when I will sell out." Obviously this type of strategy works well when you are trying to take advantage of bigger market moves and when there has been a meaningful move in your favor already.

The disadvantage of increasing your stop-loss orders in this fashion is twofold. First, you will never get out at the top of any move. With the limit order discussed immediately above this might be possible. For instance, if the market again is now 171 and you put in a limit order to sell at 173, that might be very close to the high for the day or the week. On the other hand, when you put in a stop-loss order at 169, you know in advance that that cannot be the high because you are deliberately placing it below even the current market, to say nothing of the future price. So the first disadvantage is that you will not get the high, and the second is that stop-loss orders have a habit of being touched off more often than not. With the extreme volatility of the stock-index-futures market, do not be surprised if during the afternoon for some unknown reason your contract price suddenly falls by almost 2 points, kicks off your stop-loss order and then equally inexplicably rises right back up again to where it was and proceeds to go even higher. Such are the risks of stop-loss orders.

A FLEXIBLE STRATEGY

The purpose of this book is not to lay down a hard-and-fast "system" that will work under all circumstances but rather to tell you the options available and then to present the pros and cons of each one. Here your strategy will be determined by what you are trying to accomplish. If you are interested in taking a lot of quick profits, then you are better off using a limit order. The volatility of the stock-index-futures market is working for you in this case. That is to say, that if a contract typically trades within a 3-point range during a day, you can put in a sell order at a point 1 or 2 points above the opening price with a fair degree of likelihood that it will go off during the day, giving you a nice return for one day's trading if it does. If your objectives are to go for the big hit, then you will use the method of increasing your stop-loss orders as the market goes in your favor, even though there is the chance that initially you will be shut out at the low for the day and receive little or no profit from the trade.

THE NEED TO TAKE PROFITS

But whatever method you choose, the underlying principle is the same: You must take profits. This is an imperative, and it is just as important as the first fundamental rule we learned in this chapter, which is that you must protect yourself from large losses. The reason that you must take profits, the proverb about letting your winnings run notwithstanding, is that sooner or later every rally and every decline end. At the risk of stating the obvious, let's recall that throughout the long course of the world's history there has never been a rally which did not come to an end, and there has never been a decline which did not come to an end. And I am willing to go way out on a limb and predict that the next rally or decline you are in is also not going to go on forever. The point is that we all know these truisms, yet so often we do not take advantage of them. While everyone knows that these are true, many people frequently forget that market changes in direction usually come sooner, with more suddenness and with much more force than market participants expect.

If you are not ready to take your profits with a predetermined strategy, you can all too easily see these profits disappear completely. Perhaps there is no better example of this than during July and early August 1982, when the market had been falling for about four weeks, and the Dow Jones Industrial Average finally fell below 800. The economy was clearly in very bad shape, and even though interest rates recently had fallen dramatically, this didn't make any difference to the market, which just kept going down. At that point the shorts all had wonderful profits, yet few of them took profits or even had plans to take profits in case of a market change. It was clear to them that nothing could turn the market around, and the only question on their minds was whether the Dow Jones would fall another 30 points down to 750, as most people expected, or would go down much farther, to 700 or 650, as many pessimists thought. All this pessimism led to the futures selling at large discounts to the price of the indexes, which greatly increased the short profits. And why not? There was absolutely no reason to think that the market could go up.

It was then that Henry Kauffman, the economist at Salomon Brothers, reversed his position and said that while he had previously stated repeatedly that interest rates would soon be going back to as high as they had been a year earlier, he now believed that they would continue to go down. The next day the market went up 38 points on the DJIA, and within a week it had spurted up 100 points. How many of those shorts got out in time? How many of them saw their bountiful gains converted into major losses?

Granted, most changes in direction are not nearly that dramatic. Nevertheless, the principle is the same in every minor rally that fades and every small correction that becomes a rally. When the market is going up, it always looks as if it will continue to go up, and when it comes down, there is the perception that it will keep on coming down. We must all learn that this is a natural trait of human psychology, to accept what we see and rationalize that it is correct. If the market is coming down, we say, "Of course the market is coming down, with all the trouble in the Middle East, the recession (or inflation), etc.," and when it is going up, we say, "Of course the market is going up, with all those rosy expectations for corporate earnings in the coming quarters." What we fail to realize is that even when the market was going down, there were rosy earnings forecasts, and even when it was going up, there was trouble in the Middle East. It is not the news that influences the market as much as the perception of what aspects of the news are determinative. This can change in a moment, and it usually does. Either you take your profits, or they will take their leave of you.

One of the saddest stories I've ever heard on Wall Street (and there are many sad ones) is of the former General Motors executive who was smart enough to sense that in 1929 the stock market was way overpriced. He was one of the few people smart enough to sell out in early 1929 with a good profit. Then, when the market had gone down in the great crash of 1929, he came back in and bought stocks at a small fraction of the prices they had been trading at earlier. And do you know what happened? He then went almost bankrupt in the market decline of 1932. Who would believe that such a thing could happen? But it did. The moral is that even when prices are low, you cannot be sure they will not go much lower, or vice versa. Plan in advance to take your profits.

PICKING YOUR STRATEGIES

Presented in outline form on pages 90-93 are two strategies. Your actual plan will be a combination of various features from the different strategies. Obviously, the prices are only guides which you should adjust to the correct price of your future, and you may decide that for your own purposes you want to set the buy-and-sell prices and the stop-loss prices much farther from the current market prices than is indicated in the examples.

These strategies pertain to someone who believes that the market is going up, so he takes a long position. These strategies work just as well when one is taking the short position, if you will just convert every buy order into a sell and turn the profits and losses upside down.

In actual practice few experienced futures traders use strategies as structured as the ones outlined. What happens is that a trader talks with his broker and says, "It looks as if the market is falling. Sell my five December contracts at the market, quick!" That trader couldn't tell you when he put in the order whether he will average down or pyramid up, nor will he be likely to put in a stop-loss order or a limit order to get out. But if he is experienced, in his subconscious he knows all these things. If the market suddenly starts going up, you will be amazed at how quickly he buys in his positions. He is doing this from years of experience. But in your case the way to operate is to put in a stop-loss order in advance rather than waiting until the market turns against you. Even though experienced traders might not have a fully written out strategy when they take on their initial positions, they do have such a plan in the back of their mind. For you it is a very worthwhile exercise, and actually a necessity, to have your plan carefully written out in advance. After a few months if you feel comfortable with the market and know what you will do in advance, then you can loosen the rules and operate a little more "by the seat of your pants" as you go along. For the beginning, that could well be fatal. Prepare your plan first, and put it in writing.

STICK WITH YOUR PLAN!

One final comment. The only thing worse than not having a plan at all is to have a plan and then not follow it. Before you say that this won't happen to you, let me explain just how tempting it can be not to follow a plan. Probably the most difficult temptation is the simple measure of taking your losses with a stop-loss order. To understand the emotional pull, let's take an example as it might happen to you. After a lot of study and thought you decide that the market right now is overbought and is due for a serious correction downward. You short a contract at 155. The market continues up, and you short another one at 160. You don't want to be short more than two contracts, so you figure that you should enter a stop-loss order to buy one of them at 165 and the other at 170. The market continues to move against you, and the first stop-loss order goes off at 165, giving you a loss of $5,000. Now the market moves up some more. At this point you begin to think that the market is more overbought than ever, that the fact it has gone up so much means that when the turn comes it will be much sharper and longer lasting than even you had expected and that at this really extremely overbought level it can't be a matter of more than a few days at the most before it breaks. Furthermore, if you let your second stop-loss order go off, you are realizing a loss of another $5,000, and even worse, you will be out of the market when the next downturn comes, which could put you on your way to becoming a rich man. Therefore, with all these considerations, you conclude that in the interests of prudence you should cancel your stop-loss orders, to stay in for just a little bit longer. Yes, that's just how it happens. And what happens after that?

I don't know, but I do know if you had done that in early September 1982 after the market had spurted up over 100 points on the Dow Jones (it just had to go back down after that, right?), you would have lost a lot of money as it then continued on up for another 150 points!

Don't change plans in midstream! The whole point of having a plan is that you are able to map out your strategy in advance when you can be calm, analytical and objective. You give the plan everything you have and pick the buy-and-sell levels which give you the best odds to make money consistent with your goals and objectives. Once you have done that, the chances of your being able to improve upon it when you are under the pressure and emotional tension of losing are very slight. In probably 90% of the cases, what passes for a change in a plan is nothing more than wishful thinking. Yes, wouldn't it be nice if the market would suddenly reverse itself and go your way for a change. And wouldn't it be nice if Santa Claus would come down my chimney this Christmas and give me a new Mercedes 340 SL. But unfortunately we live in a hard, cold, real world with a real market which doesn't give a damn about what would be nice for you. Follow your plan, and if it means taking a loss, so be it. That is not the end of the world. You will then be in a position to make a clearheaded, objective decision of whether you want to come back into the market.

INTRODUCTION TO TWO STRATEGIES
Described below are two strategies of the type any trader might work out for himself. It hardly needs repetition that no strategy can make money under any and all market circumstances. If there were such a plan, it would be clear that we could all become millionaires within a few weeks, and poverty on this planet could be abolished for all time. The last time I looked there were still a few non-millionaires around, even among those who have read many books on how to trade commodities. So the best we can expect from a strategy is to have a plan which will minimize our loss, or at least constrain us to a predetermined level of loss if we are wrong on our outlook of the market, and which will allow us to make a generous level of profits if we are correct on our view of the market.

The first strategy presented here is for someone who wants to be a short-term trader, going in and out on short term, small price moves within a broad trading range. His basic strategy is to buy on dips and sell on rallies. Since he does not believe the market is going to make a large move either up or down, he does not protect himself with stop-loss orders. Rather, he takes advantage of lower prices to buy more positions at lower prices, and he takes advantage of higher prices to sell more contracts at even higher prices. In our example the strategy starts with the futures contract at 150 and should work well for any price ranges between 140 and 160. When stripped of all its detail, the strategy is really one of averaging down and averaging up. As is pointed out in the outline, the difficulty comes when the futures go below 140 or over 160, and at that point I suggest that the regular strategy be abandoned and the trader begin to utilize stop-loss orders to get out of what could become a very dangerous position. When a person starts out with one view of the market—here that it will continue to trade in a range of 140 to 160—and then it breaks out of that range, it is time to change strategies and recognize the fact that you were wrong.

The second strategy is for a trader who believes there will be a major market move—in this case, on the upside. His objective is not to make money on small market moves but rather to protect himself from major losses so that when the big up moves take place he will be ready to climb on the rocket ship. Thus the strategy is complete with stop-loss orders so that he will not lose money in case the market goes down sharply. The other major contrast with the first strategy is that here one is not afraid to buy when the market goes up. In fact, the second trader is delighted to buy at ever higher prices, because this is an indication to him that the big move is under way. In this respect, he is exactly the opposite from the short-term trader who always sold on higher prices. The weakness of this strategy is that if the market begins to move up far enough so that he has bought major positions, and then turns around and goes down, he will end up with losses. In essence this strategy is one of pyramiding, and therefore, as the outline notes, one must definitely stop adding to the positions at some predetermined point on the upside.

A STRATEGY FOR A SHORT-TERM TRADER

Objective: To make money on short-term daily or weekly moves in the market. Assumptions: The market is not going to make a major move either up or down. If it does, the trader is prepared to take a substantial loss.

To read the outline, go from the notation of the order executed, to the next numbered step with the same notation. Thus if the order mentioned in 2.B was executed, go to 3.B to learn next directions.

Note: Where two orders are entered simultaneously, when one is executed, the other should be canceled. When moving to the next step, all previously entered numbers are to be canceled.

Step

1. Futures contract at 150. Enter orders to (A) buy 1 contract at 148 and (B) sell 1 at 152.

2.A If bought at 148, enter orders to buy 1 at 146 and to sell 1 at 150.

2.B If sold at 152, enter orders to buy 1 at 150 and to sell 1 at 154.

3.A If bought at 146, enter orders to buy 1 at 144 and to sell 2 at 149.

3.A If sold at 150, repeat step 1, with the possibility of increasing the quantity of contracts.

3.B If bought at 150, repeat step 1, with the possibility of increasing the quantity.

3.B If sold at 154, enter orders to buy 2 at 151 and sell 1 at 156.

4.A If bought at 144, enter orders to buy 1 at 142 and sell 3 at 148.

4.A If sold at 149, repeat step 1, using the price of 149 as the mid-price.

4.B If bought 2 at 151, repeat step 1, using 151 as the midprice.

4.B If sold at 156, enter orders to buy 3 at 152 and sell 1 at 158.

5.A If bought at 142, enter orders to buy 1 at 140 and sell 4 at 147.

5.A If sold 3 at 148, repeat step 1, using 148 as the midprice.

5.B If bought 3 at 152, repeat step 1, using 152 as the midprice.

5.B If sold 1 at 158, enter orders to buy 4 at 153 and sell 1 at 160.

6.A If bought 1 at 140, this process can continue indefinitely, but eventually if the contract price continues down, the losses and margin requirements are so great that one must cease. Therefore one should have a predetermined lower level, such as 140, at which one stops buying more contracts and uses staggered stop-loss sell orders at lower prices to limit further losses and get out.

6.A If sold at 147, repeat step 1, using 147 as the midprice.

6.B If bought 4 at 153, repeat step 1, using 153 as the midprice.

6.B If sold 1 at 160, this process can continue indefinitely if the future continues rising. Eventually as the future rises farther the losses on existing short positions and margin requirements become too great to sustain. Therefore, one should have a

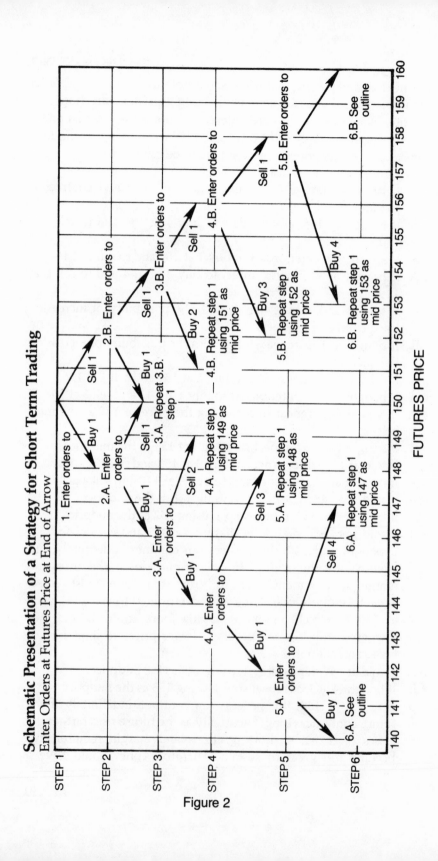

Figure 2

predetermined upper price, such as 160, at which one stops shorting more contracts and uses staggered stop-loss buy orders to limit further losses and get out.

A STRATEGY FOR A TRADER EXPECTING A MAJOR MOVE

Objective: To catch a forthcoming major move, and to do this, to be willing to accept small losses and miss small trading profits. Assumption: There will be a major move of such size that it can bring profits much greater than any short-term trading. In this example the trader is bullish, but by reversing the orders, the strategy will work equally well for a bearish trader.

Step

1. Futures contract at 150. Enter order to buy 1 at 152 on a stop.

2.A If bought 1 at 152, enter stop-loss order to sell 1 at 150, and buy order for 2 on a 154 stop.

2.B If order in step 1 is not executed before future goes down to 148, reduce stop-loss price to 150 and continue reducing stop-loss price for every 2-point decline of the future until order is executed. Then proceed as in step 2.A, using the price just paid as the basis for new orders.

3. If stop-loss order is executed at 150, repeat step 1.

3. If bought 2 at 154, retain original stop-loss order and enter stop-loss order to sell 1 at 152, and 1 at 151, and enter order to buy 4 at 156.

4. If stop-loss orders are executed, go back to step 1 for each stop-loss order, using the price of the execution in place of 150.

4. If bought 4 at 156, retain previous stop-loss orders and enter stop-loss order to sell 2 at 154 and 2 at 153 and to buy 8 at 158 stop.

5. If stop-loss orders are executed, go back to step 1 for each stop-loss order executed, using the price of the executions in place of 150.

5. If bought 8 at 158 retain all previous stop-loss orders and enter stop-loss order to sell 4 at 156 and 4 at 155. *Do not enter any additional buy orders.*

6. If any stop-loss orders are executed, go back to step 1 for each stop-loss order executed, using the price of the executions in place of 150. If the future moves up to 160, increase all stop-loss orders by 2 points. Continue to increase stop-loss orders every time the future moves by another 2 points.

93

(See figure 3 on next page.)

Schematic Presentation of a
Strategy for a Major Market Move

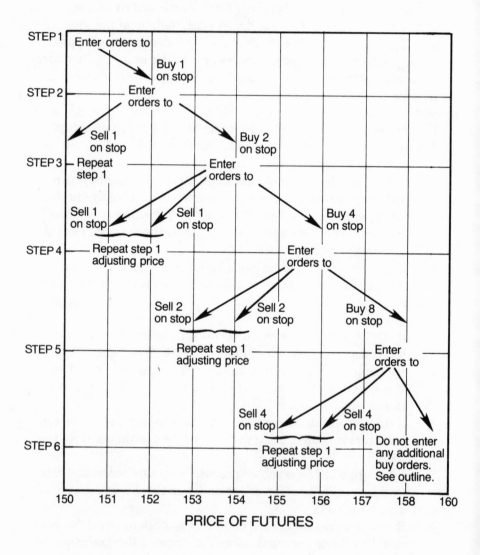

Figure 3

CHAPTER 4
Complex Trading Strategies

This chapter concerns strategies which are not necessarily difficult to comprehend, but rather strategies in which stock-index futures are used in conjunction with some other type of investment or another stock future. While by far the greatest use which will be made of stock futures will be for simple speculation as to whether the market will go up or down, they also have very beneficial uses with other investments, either as a way of creating more leverage or of providing a hedge. Another use of combining various investments is that you can make money from a relative change in two securities, regardless of their absolute moves. For example, you might not know whether the stock market is going to go up or down, but you do believe that regardless of what happens, the financial firms (banks, insurance companies, and savings and loan associations) are going to do worse than stocks in general. In this case, by going long a general index, such as the S&P 500, and shorting a financial index, you can screen out changes in stock prices in general and make money from your expectation that the financial stocks will do worse than stocks as a whole.

HEDGING A STOCK PORTFOLIO

In this section we will discuss how to protect a stock portfolio from anticipated declines in the stock market. Normally, if one expects the stock market to turn down, one would simply sell out his stock portfolio, wait for the down turn to occur and then buy back the stocks at the lower price. In practice there may be a number of reasons why this is not desirable. The first reason why you may not want to sell would be to avoid taxes. Let us assume that you have owned stock for a shorter period of time than qualifies for long-term capital gain and you believe that even though the market is headed down temporarily, you want to hang onto the stock for a few weeks more

95

until it qualifies for long-term capital gain. During this interval, however, you don't want to suffer if it goes down. Another case involving taxes arises where you have long-term stock that has such a very low tax basis that you will probably never sell it, because the taxes would be enormous. Another reason you may want to hold onto your portfolio is to avoid commissions, which on stock transactions are relatively high. If you sell your stocks, but believe the coming dip will be short-lived, you will find yourself wanting to buy the stocks back soon and will have to pay the high commissions twice. In other cases, where you have large holdings in a stock there may be a liquidity problem—if you try to sell all your stock at once, your stock coming on the market will itself depress the price of the stock even farther. For any or all of these reasons, it may be desirable, when you believe that the market is about to turn down, not to sell your stock but to take alternative means to protect your investment.

Shorting the right number of the right stock futures can give you the downside protection you are seeking. The two questions you have to decide are which index to short and how many contracts to trade. The question of which index will usually be answered by using the New York Stock Exchange or the Standard & Poor's 500 if you have a typical portfolio containing sizable positions of the large-capitalization stocks. If, however, you have mainly smaller stocks, then you should use the VLCA. If you are hedging just one stock, then of course you may be able to find a group index which will include your stocks' industry.

Choosing the Number of Contracts. The question of how many contracts is a bit more complicated. The first part of that is simply to make sure you are hedging the right amount of stock. For example, let's assume your stock portfolio is now worth $500,000. You want a complete hedge, or as near one as possible, understanding that a hedge is never perfect and your particular stocks could always decline while the market as a whole went up, which means that you would lose both on your portfolio and on the hedge as well. If you want to use the S&P, and the S&P Index is now at 145, then you would multiply the index by $500 to determine that shorting one contract of the S&P is the equivalent of shorting $72,500 worth of stock. Dividing $72,500 into the amount of your portfolio, we determine that you would need to short seven contracts to hedge yourself against losses. That is to say, if you have shorted seven contracts and your stocks roughly match those in the S&P Index, then for every $1 you lose in your stocks, you should make $1 on your short contracts. If you are wrong and the stock market goes up, then every $1 you make on your stocks will be offset by a loss of $1 on your indexes.

For very large portfolios, another step is indicated. This is to determine what the Beta of your portfolio is. By Beta we mean the tendency of your portfolio to move with the market. If it tends to move at the same rate as the market it would have a Beta of 1, and if it tends to move more than the market as a whole it would have a Beta of perhaps 1.5. Both the S&P and the NYSE indexes have Betas of about 1. If your portfolio has a Beta of 1.5, then you will need about 50% more contracts to give you a mathematically equal hedge; if your Beta is much lower, you will need fewer contracts. The actual number can be worked out only by obtaining the Beta for each stock in your portfolio and thus determining the weighted Beta of your entire portfolio.

Hedging a Specific Stock. Suppose you learn good news about a particular company which will cause it to rise relative to the market. You are interested in acquiring a goodly position of its stock. But you are worried that the stock market as a whole may be heading for a fall which would drag this stock down with it. Heretofore you might simply not have bothered acquiring the stock. But with the advent of stock futures you now have a way to cancel out the effect of the market as a whole on this particular stock. By shorting the number of contracts of stock futures required to offset the value of the stock you are acquiring, and adjusting if necessary for the Beta of the stock you are acquiring, you are able to reduce greatly the loss you will suffer from the fact that the market as a whole may decline. Then, if the stock you bought declines less on a percentage basis than the market as a whole, you will still make money.

SPREADS BETWEEN INDEXES

There is no way to make as much money quickly as there is to be correct about which way the market will move and being long or short one of the futures. But oftentimes we do not have firm convictions about the market as a whole. We may, however, have convictions about different groups of stocks relative to the movement of the market as a whole. For example, if we believe that the oil stocks will underperform the market in the coming months, we still may not feel like betting that the oil stocks will go down, because if the entire market is swept up in a rush of bullishness, it will undoubtedly carry the oils along with it to some extent. We want to find a technique which will enable us to make money from the relative decline of the oils in relation to the market as a whole. Or perhaps we believe that the computer stocks are ready for a real move up, but that if an economic recession comes on which would take the entire stock market down with it, even the computer stocks would go down, although probably not as much as the market as a whole.

The answer to these investing needs is the spread in which we go long or short one stock-index future, and do the opposite with another one. In the first example above, you would short the petroleum group index, then cancel out the effect of a possible market rise by going long one of the stock market indexes. Thus, even if the stock market went up, you would still make money, provided only that the oil stocks did not go up by as much as the market as a whole. Of course, if the market stayed still and the oil stocks declined, you would pick up your profit on the oil stocks. In brief, as long as the oil stocks do not do as well as the stock market as a whole, it does not matter to you whether the market goes up, goes down or stays still. Your spread has canceled out the effect of a general market move and enabled you to make money by the precise conviction you have, namely that the oil stocks would underperform the market.

In the second example, you would go long the computer group index, then short the general market index. This would cancel out the negative effect which a stock market decline would have on the computer stocks. Once you had put on this spread, the market could go up, down or sideways and you would still make money, provided only that the computer group outperformed the stock market in general.

Having Equal Value on Both Sides. The possibilities are almost limitless, and the only real difficulty comes in making sure that you have approximately equal values of stock on the two sides and that you also consider any major differences in Betas between the two indexes.

Most of the spreads will be between one of the group indexes and another group index or a market index, but occasionally you might want to spread the market indexes themselves. If you believed that the blue-chip, large-capitalization stocks such as IBM, General Motors, Eastman Kodak and General Electric had already had their run-up, were now due for a rest and that the next market move would come in the smaller, second-tier stocks, but you didn't want to assume the risk that the entire market might go down, you would want to go long the VLCA and short either the NYSE or the S&P 500. To give yourself a 100% hedge you would have to be certain that the amount of stock represented by the contracts you were long was equal to the amount of the stock you were short. Otherwise you would have a bias to your hedge, which might be all right, but you should at least be certain in the beginning that you know what it is. For example, at one time when the March VLCA was 161, the S&P was 141. This means that a hedge of one contract against one of the others would give you a 14% greater weight to the VLCA. This is great if the market moves in the direction of the VLCA, but if it goes in the other direction you will lose money you didn't expect to lose.

Spreading a Group Index Against a Market Index. When spreading one of the group indexes against one of the regular market indexes (or against another group index, for that matter), you will have to be more careful to keep the two sides of the spread even. For example, at one time the NYSE Financial Group March contract was 92.60, while the NYSE Index March contract was 81.70. It seems like a pretty close hedge until we remember that the NYSE Financial Index has a value of $1,000 for every point move. Thus one contract on the Financial Index represents $92,600 of stock, while a contract on the NYSE Index represents only $40,850 worth of stock. So you would have to use at least two contracts of the market indexes to come close to one contract of the financial indexes.

If you are trying to get a real hedge which will eliminate the effect of a general market move on what you are doing, you also will have to give effect to the Betas of the contracts with which you are working. For instance, computer stocks are inherently more volatile than the market as a whole. Suppose you believe they will go up but you want to filter out the risk of a general market decline. You go long enough contracts of the computer group so that they represent about the same value of stock you are shorting in one of the general market indexes. If you are right and the market goes up, you will probably make money because the computer stocks will move up by a greater percentage than the market as a whole. But if the market goes down, your computer stocks will probably go down at a faster rate than the market as a whole and you will be losing money. The point is that if you are trying to achieve a hedge you should strive to have contracts on both sides which will probably gain or lose an equal actual dollar amount from a general market rise or fall. And the amount of the expected rise or fall in the value of a portfolio, index or group is determined by the amount of the portfolio multiplied by the amount of gain or loss in the market and by the Beta of that group.

CHAPTER 5
Options on Indexes

What is the difference between going long a future contract on an index and buying a call option on that index? This must be one of the most frequently asked questions of any broker who deals in the indexes. The person asking the question probably knows that they are both highly leveraged and that they can both make a lot of money if the market goes up. But there the similarity ends.

The very basic difference is that going long a future contract on an index is like taking a position in that index. You do not actually own a share of the index, but the practical effect is the same. When the contract goes in your direction you make money, and when it goes down you lose money, almost point for point with the underlying index. Because you have taken a position in the index, you are obligated to do something eventually to get out of your position. Even if you wait until the contract expires and do nothing, your brokerage firm will do something for you. It will finally settle the future at the price of the underlying index. In a futures contract your potential loss is unlimited if you are going short, and if you are going long the loss is limited only by the price of the index. To sum up going long or short a futures contract, you are right in the action and for most purposes can consider yourself as "owning" a futures index worth $500 a point.

OPTIONS COMPARED WITH FUTURES

A person who buys a call option on an index is actually one step farther removed from owning anything. He has not taken a position in that index but has bought the right to take a position at some future date if he wishes to do so. The person who goes long or short a future is living in the present. His account is marked to the market every day by his brokerage firm, which means that money is coming into his account or going out daily. The person who buys an option is not marked to the market. He merely owns a right, which fluctuates in value daily, but it is like being told that the value of your house went up or down last month. It doesn't make any difference to you until the time comes to sell it. One of the big differences is that the owner of a call option has no obligations of any kind. He has bought a one-way ticket running in his favor. He can never be asked to put up more money, he can never be made to exercise his option, there is no detriment whatsoever that he can ever incur by virtue of owning that call other than losing his original purchase cost. The person who has a position on a futures contract can be forced to put up more money every day until he finally closes out his position.

Call Options Defined. There are similarities, of course. On a daily basis, certain options may move in close parallel to the futures—that is for every point increase in the underlying index, both the call options and the futures may move up approximately a point. And the reverse is true on the downside. So from this limited perspective, they are alike. But the differences are also great, and a consideration of them will convince many people who are not willing to take the risks of futures that options offer the kind of speculative instrument they are looking for. First let's describe what a call option is. It is the right to buy one contract of a named future or named index at a given price within a given period of time. Now we'll discuss each of these terms.

First, the option is merely a right. It is not in itself a piece of property in the normal sense. In itself it is nothing but the right to acquire a stock-index-futures contract, or the value of a stock index which does have value.

Second, the optionholder has the right to acquire the named future or index at a fixed price. That price is called the strike price or the exercise price. It is this price which gives the call option its value, because if the contract or the index is selling for a price above the strike price of the option, then the option will have a value at least equal to the difference between the two. For example, if the June futures contract is at 162 and you own the June 160 call on that future, then you have the right to acquire that future for 160, which means you will get a discount of 2 points. In other words, you could buy the contract for 160 by using your call, then immediately sell it on the futures exchange for 162. This will give you a 2-point profit. This means that your call will be worth 2 points. To determine how much this is actually worth, multiply it by $500 to get $1,000. The higher the price of the futures contract is above the strike price of your call, the greater the value of your call will be. If the contract moved up to 164, then using your call to buy the contract at 160 would give you a discount of 4 points, or $500 times that for $2,000. So it is the level of the strike price in relation to the price of the futures contract which gives the call its value.

Finally, the expiration date of the call is extremely important in determining its value. The options on stock-index futures all expire on the same day as the underlying futures contracts. Options are limited in time, and once their expiration date has passed, they become totally worthless. Futures contracts also become worthless once they have expired, but the distinction is that as the futures contract gets closer to the expiration date, its price becomes closer and closer to the price of the actual stock index, and as we know, on the final date of the futures life, it is given the exact price of the index itself. This is not true for a call option, whose price can fluctuate wildly and may bear little relationship to the price of the contract.

OPTIONS ON FUTURES
COMPARED TO OPTIONS ON INDEXES

There are two basic types of options on stock indexes. One is an option on a stock-index-futures contract and the other is an option on the index itself. The options on the S&P 500, the NYSE Index and the Value Line Composite Average are all options on the futures contract. This means that the owners of a call option on one of these indexes have the right to acquire an actual futures contract on the index for the month of the option. For example, if you buy a June 150 call option on the S&P 500, this means that if you exercise your call, you will become the owner of a June S&P 500 futures contract and will have bought it at 150. You can then either sell the contract for whatever its market price happens to be then, or you can continue to hold it.

The other type of options are the options on the indexes themselves, such as options on the CBOE-100, the Major Market Index and the subgroup indexes of the various stock exchanges. Since there is no way actually to own an index, there was no way that exercise of an option on an index could be satisfied by delivery of an index. Therefore, all options on indexes are satisfied upon exercise by a cash settlement equal to the closing price of the index on the previous day. For example, if you own a September 140 call on the CBOE-100 and you exercise it, you will be acquiring the index for 140, but your account will be treated as if you acquired it for that amount and then sold it at the closing price on the day of your exercise. If the index closed at 150 on the day you exercised the option, your account would be credited with the difference between the two of 10 points, multiplied by $100 (which is the factor for the CBOE-100), giving you a credit of $1,000.

The difference between these two types of options can be important. First, the options on futures tend to move up and down by wider amounts than the options on the indexes, because these options are priced on the basis of the futures, and the futures tend to move with greater swings than the indexes. Second, most brokerage firms insist that a customer have a commodity account to trade options on futures. As mentioned previously, the financial suitability requirements for having a commodities account can be quite high. Options on indexes, on the other hand, are traded in a regular stock account, and anyone who qualifies to buy a regular stock option can purchase an option on an index. The third difference is that a person exercising an option on an index terminates his speculation, because it has been reduced to solid cash, whereas the person who exercises an option on a future is still involved in a speculation similar to the one he was in before, except that it is now in the form of a futures contract instead of an option. This may mean that he will now have to add more money to his account to cover the margin requirement on the future.

OPTION PRICES

To illustrate how option prices move, let's assume you own a call on a future and the call has a 160 strike price and the futures contract is currently 155. The call option will have no value at all if it is almost 4:00 P.M. EST on the last day of its life. Let's consider why this is true. Here we have an option which gives its owner the right to acquire a futures contract for 160, and this is the last day in which you can take advantage of this right. The futures contract itself is selling for 155 on the futures exchange. This means that anyone can acquire the contract for 155. Your guaranteed right under your call to acquire it for 160 is therefore totally worthless. In fact, even if the price of the futures contract were 160, and it were the final minute of the day in the call's life, the call would be worthless, because anyone could buy the futures contract for the same price without the option as he could with the option. Therefore, the option confers nothing of value and is worthless. The conclusion is that at least in its final day, for an option to have any value the price of the futures contract, or index, must be above the exercise or strike price of the call option.

Once the price of the futures contract goes above the exercise or strike price of the call option it does have value, and its price on the last day will reflect that fact. As mentioned above, the value of the call on its last day will always be approximately equal to the difference between the price of the contract and the exercise price of the call.

Puts Defined. Now that we have described call options, let's talk about the other kind of options: puts. Whereas you buy a call when you believe that an index is about to go up, you buy a put when you think it is going to go down. When you own a put option, you have the right to sell the index, or a future on the index, for a given price within a given period of time. Like the call option, a put option is not any property in itself but merely gives the owner a right to do something which might be of value. In the case of the put, he has the right to sell the underlying security for a set price called the strike price. Since a put gives its owner the right to sell at this price, the higher the strike price of a put is, the greater value the put will have and the higher the price of the put will be. As with a call, the life of a put is strictly limited by its expiration date, and it expires totally and completely on that expiration date. The expiration dates of puts are identical to those of calls, and the strike prices are set at the same levels as for the calls.

Now let's take an example of just how a put might work in practice. Let's say that a futures contract is at 165 and there is a put on the future which has a strike price of 160 which will expire in three months. The current price of that put is 2. Once you buy the put for 2, you have the right at any time between now and the expiration date of the put to sell the future for 160. At the present time you would not do that, because the future itself is worth 165 and therefore you could sell it for that much. Selling it for 160 through your put would result in your receiving 5 points less than you would in the free market and therefore makes no sense. You bought the put because you believe that at some time before its expiration the future will be selling below 160. Let's assume you are right and within a few weeks the market plunges to 155. Through your put, you have the right to "sell" the future for 160. If you exercised your put, you would thus sell the future for 160. If you had no prior position in the future you would therefore be short one future with a sale price of 160. You would then purchase a future on the open market for its current price of 155, thus closing out your position, resulting in a profit on the exercise of 5 points. Since you originally paid 2 points to purchase the put, your profit on the entire transaction would be 3 points. In actual practice, it might be advisable simply to sell the put rather than exercise the put and purchase a contract. Since it is not possible actually to buy or sell an index, all options on indexes themselves (as distinct from futures on indexes) are exercised for cash, as if you had sold the index for cash.

The same basic rules apply to puts as apply to calls. If at the expiration date of the put, the index or the future is not below the strike price of the put, then the put will be worthless, and the entire amount you spent to purchase it will be lost. Second, the longer the duration of the put, the more expensive it will be. And finally, the higher the strike price, the more the put will be worth.

Volatility of Options. To explain the extreme volatility of a call option in comparison to the price fluctuation of the futures contract itself, consider another example. Let's say the futures contract is at 160. The 160 call would be practically worthless on the last day. Now the contract makes a very small advance, to 160.50. This is an increase of 0.3% in the price of the index, and anyone who had laid down $6,000 in margin to go long one contract would have an unrealized profit of $0.50 times 500, or $250 per contract, which is a gain of 4.1% on his investment.

Now let's look at the option. When the contract was 160, the 160 call actually had no intrinsic value, but let's assume it was selling at about $0.25 toward the end of the last day. When the contract moved up to 160.50, the option was now worth $0.50, which means that there was an increase of $0.25. Multiplying by $500, we find that the contract has gone from being worth $125 to being worth $250. This represents an increase in the price of the call of 100%. This is what I mean by saying that the prices of calls can change by extremely large amounts, with no direct relationship to the percentage changes in the contracts themselves. Here is a great example of that. A change of 4.1% for anyone who was long the futures contract is translated into a change of 100% for a person who owned the call contract.

Before you rush to cash in all you futures contracts for call options, consider one not-so-minor point. It works the other way, too.

Suppose you are interested in the contract just mentioned, which is now selling for 160.50 because you believe it is very likely to go higher. You go long the contract. Your friend, having just read the above paragraphs, decides there is no need to tie up $6,000 of capital in the hope of making a relatively small profit. So he purchases the call option for $0.50, which is $250. Unfortunately for both of you, the market does something totally unexpected (at least by each of you) and has the nerve actually to go down instead of up. It closes the day at 160. You have a loss in your futures contract of $250, which represents a decrease in your investment of 4.1%, whereas the call contract ends the day absolutely worthless, for a loss of $250 to your friend, but this represents a 100% loss to him. You both lost the same amount of dollars in this example, but only because you were playing with about twenty-four times as much money. If your friend had decided to buy $6,000 worth of options, he would have lost $6,000 on that day's move compared to your loss of $250. This shows you what I mean by extreme price changes.

The different strike prices of options also gives them a marked difference from the futures contract. There is only one price for the June contract on any index. If you want to go long, you have no choice as to what kind of leverage you can get. The futures contract is very standard, and the cost of playing the game is the amount of margin required. With options, you have quite a choice of the type of leverage you want to give yourself. In the case of futures, it is easy to divide the value of the underlying index itself by the amount of margin required to determine the amount of leverage you have. For instance, if a futures contract requires $6,000 in initial margin and the contract is selling for 140 so that it is worth $70,000, then you have leverage of 11.66 to 1. With options you have a choice of leverage because the options at each different strike price have a different amount of leverage.

Let's take some examples where the index is selling for 150. In the same expiration period, there is a 145 strike-price call selling for 8, a 150 strike-price call selling for 4 and a 155 strike-price call selling for 2. Which offers the most leverage, and how can you figure it out? One way to go about this is to estimate what change will take place in the options' prices for a specific move in the price of the index between now and the expiration date. Let's start by assuming that the index moves up to 165 on the expirations date. At that point the 145 option will enable the owner to acquire the index for 145, and since it is actually worth 165, he will be saving 20, which means that the option itself will be worth 20 on expiration. The 150 option will enable its owner to acquire the contract for a savings of 15, and so it will be worth 10 by similar reasoning.

Thus we see that a move of 10 points in the underlying index produces gains of 12 points in the 145 option, which represents a gain for that option of 150%; produces a gain of 11 in the next higher strike-price option, which is a gain of 275%; and produces a gain of 8 points in the next higher strike-price option, which is a profit of 400%. The point here is that by selecting the different strike prices one is able to decide just how much leverage he wants from an option. This example shows that when the contract itself moves far enough, the call option with the highest strike price will give the biggest-percentage profits, and the one with the lowest strike price will produce the lowest-percentage profits. We'll go into certain disadvantages of the higher strike prices in greater detail later, but for now let's just note that if the contract only went to 154 when it expired, the 155 option would be worth nothing, whereas the 150 option would be worth 4, which is its break-even point, and the 145 option would be worth 9 so that it would actually show a slight profit.

Call Options vs. Futures. Now that we understand a little about call options, let's summarize just how they differ from the futures:

1. *The amount of risk is absolutely limited to the initial cost of the option.* Inherent in the basic definition of an option is that when you own a call option, you have a right to do something if you wish but have absolutely no obligation to do anything you do not wish. Clearly, you would not choose to lose more money than you originally paid. Hence there is no way that you can be made, or even asked, to send more money after you have paid the initial price of the call. You will remember that, by way of contrast, when you take on a long position in a futures contract, you lose point for point as it goes down. If you started out only with a limited amount of margin, then your brokerage firm will try to close out your account before you actually lose more money than you put up if you don't send in any more, but if there should be a large gap (big and sudden) move against you, then you are legally liable for the difference. This limited liability of the option is one of the most appealing aspects of options and one

which means that a great deal more people will want to get the benefits of indexes through options instead of through futures.

2. *The possibility of enormous leverage.* When we discussed using futures we pointed out that the margin requirements meant that you would get about a 10 to 1 leverage, meaning that a move of 1% up or down in the price of the futures contract would be equal to a gain or loss of 10% to you if you were using the minimum amount of margin. There is no such relationship when it comes to options. The amount of leverage in an option can vary by almost any amount. Under some circumstances it would be less than with a future, although this would be unusual, and in some circumstances it could be 100 to 1, provided the contract moved in the right direction and by the right amount and within the right amount of time. If you buy an option with a strike price far above the price of the index with just a short period of time to go, it will be priced so low that if the index moves over the strike price by any significant amount, you could have your leverage of 100 to 1. This will happen very infrequently. But the point here is that the leverage of options is variable, and the possibility of making a real killing with a known, limited amount of money at risk will also make trading options on indexes appealing to many people.

As an example of the leverage possible with options, let's take an example where the index you are interested in is at 145 and you decide to buy a 150 strike-price option with just a little time to go for 1 point. This will cost you $500. If the index moves by 10 points to 155, your option will be worth 5 at the expiration date. This means that you have made a profit of 4 or $2,000 on your speculation of $500, which is a profit of 400%. By way of comparison, if the futures contract had also gone from 145 to 155, an initial margin deposit of $6,000 would show a profit of 10 points, which multiplied by $500 gives an increase of $5,000, which is only 83%. There it is: 400% vs. 83%. While the difference will sometimes be the other way, this does illustrate the high profit potential of options.

3. *Lower entry cost.* The lowest margin currently available for a stock-index future is the NYSE contract, which is $3,500. Options can be purchased at whatever price they happen to be, and that may be less than $100. Therefore for the person who wants to start out in this market with a very small amount, options offer an advantage.

4. *Greater probability of losing 100% of the money put up.* This may come as a surprise, since we have been at pains to point out that with the

futures you can lose more than you originally put up. True, but in all but the most unusual cases your futures position would be closed out by stop-loss orders or by your brokerage firm long before it got to the zero figure.

In fact, if the firm did not close out your account while you still had a hefty amount of money with them, they would be derelict in their duty. No brokerage firm wants to be in a position where the customer has lost money not in his account. So, at least 99% of the time that a person trades futures, if he loses money he will still have a lot left at the end.

With options there is no such force at work. Since they are fully paid for at the outset, there is no involvement of the brokerage firm's margin department. They don't care if you lose all your money, because they know you can't lose any of their money. But on a more basic level, the reason why you are more likely to lose all your money is due to the fundamentally more risky nature of the options, particularly the out-of-the-money options. That term describes options in which the strike price is away from the current price of the future, so that only if the index moves in your direction before the option's expiration date will the option be worth anything. Thus if an index is at 133 and you buy the 135 call option, that is an out-of-the-money option because the index has to move up by 2 points before the option will be worth anything on its expiration date. If you were buying the 140 option we would say that that is a far-out-of-the-money option, and the 130 call option would be an in-the-money option. Getting back to our example, if you decide to buy the 140 call option because it is not too expensive and you believe that the market is about to have a major rally, you are going to lose all your money at the expiration date unless the index makes the move to over 140.

While this may seem like an easy thing to do, the chances of its happening and your selling out the option when the index is above 140 are not as great as you may think. But let's look at one possibility to illustrate the difference between the future and the option. Let's suppose that the index does indeed rally handsomely, right up to 145, but you believe it will go substantially higher, so you wait. It then settles down, and finally on the expiration date of the option it is at 139. This means it has gone up 6 points, which is not a bad rally. Anyone who bought the future when you did at 133 and sold out on the expiration date of your option made a profit of 6 points or

$3,000. Good for him. Now let's see just how much you made. Your option entitles you to obtain the index at a price of 140. With the index available on the floor of the futures exchange at 139, there is no benefit confirmed by your option, and therefore your option is worthless.

The point here is crucial. When you purchase out-of-the-money calls and put options, even if you are correct and the market does move in your direction, you will still lose all your money if the market doesn't move fast enough and far enough. And there is probably nothing sadder than a person who was right on the market and still loses all his money. Just imagine how you would feel. Cheated, to say the least. And of course if the market moves against you, you will also lose all your money. So if you are considering the purchase of an option, keep in mind that the odds are actually very good that your option will expire worthless.

Of course, it is always possible to sell an option before it expires, and even if the market has moved against you, the option should be worth something. But it is always psychologically difficult to sell when there is a large loss, and it may not be even the best course of action. (See the rules of strategy later in this chapter for suggestions.)

5. *Higher premium.* Futures may be selling at a premium to the price of the index, or they may be selling at a discount, but even when they are selling at a premium it is likely to be only 1 or 2 points. Options almost always trade at a premium, and it can be quite hefty. In the case of the out-of-the-money options, their entire price is always equal to the amount of the premium, since one defines premium to mean the amount by which the price of a security exceeds the actual cash value if it were to be exercised at the current price of the underlying index. This point is important because the higher premium is practically the only disadvantage options have in comparison to futures. It is, however, an extremely important one, and one which many small investors are likely to overlook to their detriment.

The effect of this premium can be seen easily in an example. Let's say the index you want to go long is now at 150. The closest expiration month has thirty days left, and the future has a 1-point premium—that is, it is at 151, whereas the 150 option is at 4. To keep the example simple, let's assume you decide to hold your speculation until the expiration date. Since the future is selling at a point over the index, this means that over the next thirty days if the index stays still you will lose a point. With the option selling at 4, you are losing 4 points if the index stays still. You are clearly playing with the odds well stacked against you. It is somewhat similar to going into a casino to play roulette. You have a choice of betting on the black or the red, but 2% of the time the ball will land on the star and neither black nor red wins, but the house picks up the chips from all players. Here when you buy the option, if nothing happens you will lose four points, and for every point gain made in the index, that gain will be subtracted from your 4-point loss. If the index goes up 4 points to 154, you are just getting even. In effect, those 4 points are just like the stars in the roulette wheel. It is the house's fee for letting you play the game. You may well believe that the game is worth the price, but you should be well aware of the cost of the game before you play.

Another way to think of the premium would be as a handicap in a race. In this case you might allegorize your purchase of the 150 option at 4 to someone who decides to enter a race and is given a starting position 4 yards behind the other runners. The effect is exactly the same. You must move 4 points just to get to the starting line. Then and only then, if you go beyond that point, will you begin to make money. You may believe that the advantages of options are so great and 4 points are so little (after all, the index can and sometimes does move that much in just a day) that you will gladly pay the price. But be aware of what you are doing. You can be sure of one thing: The person who is on the other side of the trade selling you that call option has most assuredly figured it all out, and he is very happy picking up those 4 points.

There are two reasons why you might not care about the premium at all. The first is if you are a very short-term speculator. If you intend to get in this morning and to get out by tomorrow afternoon, you won't care very much about the premium, because all things being equal, it should be just about the same tomorrow when you sell as it was when you bought today. So you won't lose much if anything. In fact, the amount of the premium might even increase, although this is unlikely. The second reason you might not care is that you are focusing exclusively on the prices of the option itself and don't give a hoot at what premium it is trading—for example, if you buy the option at 4 and have decided you will sell it if it goes down to 3 and will get out if it goes up to 7. Since you are looking at the option independently of the underlying index, you might say that it doesn't make any difference to you. But even in this case, the fact that the premium will shrink with the passage of time makes it much more difficult to sell out at a profit.

But even in these two cases, it does make a difference, to a smaller degree. When you get in and out of an option in two days, the premium has a way of shrinking dramatically when the index rises. If the index goes from 150 to 154, you are not likely to see the option go from 4 to 8. Far more likely is a move to 6 or perhaps at best 7. This factor does have an advantage when things are going against you. Let's assume that the index goes down 4 points, to 146. Your option will definitely not go down 4 points, to zero. Instead, it might only go down to about 2½ or 3.

6. *Large differences in prices for different months.* When we looked at the futures we noticed that the more distant months were almost invariably selling for higher prices than the nearer months. But the differences tend to be rather modest, frequently less than a point for a difference of three months. With the options, the differences can be very great. For example, if the near-term option has only a few weeks to go before its expiration and it is out of the money, it might be selling for only 1, but the next expiration option may be selling for 4, whereas the corresponding futures might be priced at 145.50 and 146.10. These large time premiums lead to different strategies in trading them and to paying increased attention to the different expirations. In the futures, it really didn't make a significant difference which expiration you bought, because if you bought a short-term one and it was about to expire, you could always sell it and buy a longer one for a relatively small difference in premium. But with options it can make a great deal of difference. The process of rolling over can be very expensive indeed, and therefore if you are planning to be in a position for very long you should give careful consideration to buying a longer-term option.

7. *Differences in price between puts and calls.* Futures were very simple when it came to deciding what to do when you wanted to go long or short. If you went long, you bought the futures contract at the current price, and if you wanted to go short, you sold the same contract at the same price. Obviously, with options this is vastly different. If you think the future is going to go up you buy a call, and if you think it is coming down, you buy a put. There are often large differences in the prices of these two options. Generally the call options are more expensive than the puts. There are two reasons for this. The first is

that theoretically the call buyer is buying a chance to make more money than the put buyer, since there is a limit as to how far down an index can go (somewhere above zero), but in theory there is no limit as to how high it can go. So the call buyer is really getting a bit more for his money. The second reason has to do with interest rates and the cost of money which induce institutions to buy calls and sell puts.

8. *Choice of strike prices.* If you want to take a position in the futures, you have only one price you can use, and that is the current price for whichever month happens to take your fancy. Your only choice is whether you want to go long or short that futures contract or whether you don't. With options, there is always a choice of a number of exercise prices available, which means that you can do a great deal of fine-tuning in accordance with your exact speculative goal. In general, the deeper in the money the strike price of a call option, the more expensive the call is going to be, and the more similar the purchase of an option will be actually to going long the future itself. The farther out of the money the strike price of a put or a call is, the less money you will be paying for the option and the more of a high-risk "go for broke" speculation it becomes.

This can be illustrated by assuming that the index is at 150, and the nearest term future is at the same price. You decide you want to buy a near-term option. The choices are the 140 option at 12, the 150 at 4 and the 160 at 2. We'll analyze each one under various circumstances.

In-the-Money Option. The 140 strike-price option is the most like the future itself, because its price tends to move the most like the future. If the price of the index moves down 10 points at the expiration date of the option to 140, then the option will be worth nothing and the 10-point decline in the index will be accompanied by a loss of 12 points in the option. If the contract moves up by 10 points to 160, the option at its expiration date will be at 20, which is an increase of 8 points, very nearly the same increase as the 10 points in the index. If the index moves up to any higher figure, the option will also go up point for point. On a percentage basis, these changes are much greater than for the index, of course, but not as high as for the other options. The increase of 10 points in the index leads to an increase of 8 points or 66% in the price of the option, and an increase of 20 points in the index would create an increase in the option of 18 points, for a 150% increase. On the other hand, when the index stays at the same place, the loss of 2 points is a loss of just about 17%, and a decline of 5 points to 145 would make the option 5 points for a loss of 7, or a loss of about 58%.

On-the-Money Option. Now let's look at the 150 strike-price option which was selling for 4. The first important point is that if at the expiration of the option the index is unchanged at 150, the option will be completely worthless, for a loss of 100%. This is very important, because it means (as we noted before in our discussion of premiums) that the dealer wins all ties. And while you may say that the chances of the index being absolutely unchanged are very slight, the concept carries through to other prices as well. If the index moves down, the option will also be worth nothing at expiration. If the contract moves up to 155, then the option would be worth 5 at expiration, which means there is a gain of 1 point or 20%. If the index moves up to 160, then the option becomes 10 at expiration, for a gain of 150%, and at 170 there is a gain of 16 points or 400%. You can see at a glance that the percentage gains are much greater than with the 140 option once the index goes above the 155 mark. The clear disadvantage is that for any price below 154, the losses are much greater, and as we saw, at 150 and lower the loss is 100%, whereas for the 140 call the loss at 150 was just a small 2-point, 17% loss. The higher the index goes, the greater will be the disparity in percentage gains, with the 150 option gaining at a greater and greater rate as the index goes up.

Out-of-the-Money Option. Let's consider the 160 strike-price option. This is the really volatile fellow. First we note that if the index stays still or declines at expiration of the option, it is worthless, just as it would be for the 150 strike price. But here comes more bad news. If the index moves up to 155 the option is also worthless at expiration, and if the index does really well and moves up to 160, the option is also worth nothing at expiration. Now the old saying about the dealer taking all ties takes on new meaning. Not only does the dealer get to keep all ties, but he even gets to keep the entire amount bet even if the index moves up by a full 10 points. And that is really giving away a great deal. Consider for a moment that there is almost exactly a 50% chance that the index will move down. There is another small chance that it will stay just about where it is. Therefore there is less than a 50% chance that it will move up, perhaps something like a 45% probability that it will be significantly higher at the expiration than it was when you bought the option. Of that 45%

probability, how often will it move up by a full 10 points (or in this case by about 7%, which is about equal to 70 points on the Dow Jones Industrial Average)? Without making a time-consuming survey it is impossible to come up with the exact answer, but common sense tells us that the Dow Jones doesn't move up by 70 points within a month very often—maybe only once or twice a year. This means that you have at best a chance of about one in six, about 17%. And that is not a very high rate of success, especially when you consider what will happen to you if this quite unusual event does not come about.

Getting back to our example, recall that we were discussing the purchase of the 160 strike-price call for $2 when the index was at 150. Suppose you are very lucky and the one chance in six happens and the index does move up 10 points to 160. Where exactly are we at the expiration date with our 160 call option? All that good luck and planning plus undoubtedly a lot of worry and anxiety have produced at the expiration date of the option a total wipeout. As we know, if the index is at 160 on the expiration date of the option, and its strike price is 160, then the option is worth exactly nothing. If you had bought the 160 call on the hope that the market was about to go up, and it did indeed go up to 160, you would have the satisfaction of knowing that you were right in your views of which way the market would move, you were also right in thinking it would make that move within the month and further you were also right in thinking it would make a move of some significance (in this case, a full 10 points). Unfortunately, because you picked the 160 call instead of one with a lower strike price, you would also not make any money on your speculation but actually lose it all. You get all the satisfaction of being right, but as far as it affects your bank balance, you might just as well have been dead wrong. This has to be one of the most frustrating aspects of call options, and regrettably it happens regularly to people who purchase either puts or calls.

Now for the good news (after all, there has to be a reason why people are willing to pay good money for out-of-the-money options). If the index goes up from 150 to 162 on expiration, you will break even. If it goes up to 164, your option will be worth 4 points, which means that you will have doubled your money. And after that, every time the index moves by another 2 points, you are adding another 100% of your original stake to your profits. So the great advantage of buying out-of-the-money options is that if you are right

Profit from In-the-Money, On-the-Money, and Out-of-the-Money Calls

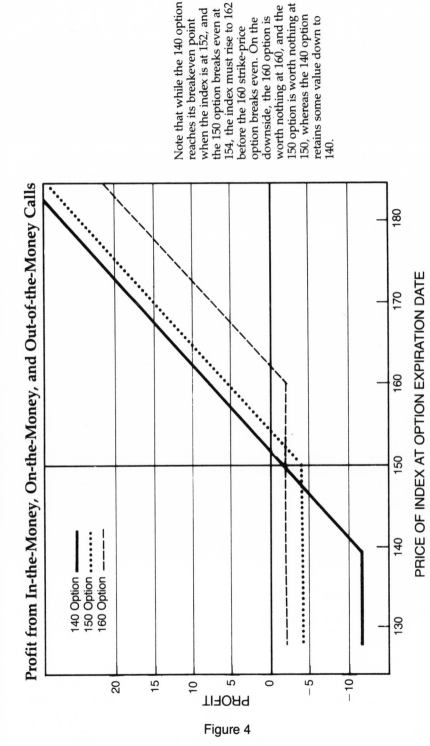

Note that while the 140 option reaches its breakeven point when the index is at 152, and the 150 option breaks even at 154, the index must rise to 162 before the 160 strike-price option breaks even. On the downside, the 160 option is worth nothing at 160, and the 150 option is worth nothing at 150, whereas the 140 option retains some value down to 140.

Figure 4

and the market does move in the direction you believe it will, and it makes that move within the time of your option, and it makes enough of a move so it goes substantially above your strike price, then you can make an enormous profit. In this example, if the index moves up to 170, your call will be worth 10 points, which means you have a profit of 8 points (400% on your investment). Interestingly enough, this is exactly the percentage profit you would receive from the 150 strike-price option when the index hits 170 at expiration of the option. The difference is that with the 160 option you are adding another 100% of profits for every additional 2-point rise in the index, whereas it takes an additional rise of 4 points to produce another 100% increase for the 150 call.

ADVANTAGES OF OPTIONS

These eight points summarize the major differences between options and futures. What the differences amount to in summary is that options represent a way to trade in the indexes with a limited capital exposure, with the potential of making a lot of money if you are right but with the overall odds less in your favor than when you take a position in a futures contract. An economist would say that your cost of playing the market via options is higher than with futures. But this is not to minimize the very real advantages options offer. They not only limit your risk but also take less capital, so they can offer greater leverage. Obviously many people are not willing to accept the risk of theoretically almost unlimited losses which the futures present. And even though I recommend using stop-loss orders to limit risks with futures, options can be superior for two reasons. The first is that there can never be complete assurance that your stop-loss order will go off near the selling price you set. As we noted before, if the price of your future gets close to your stop-loss level but doesn't quite touch it, and then on the following day gaps up on the opening by 3 points, you would be in the position of buying in your short position at almost 3 points above your limit.

The second reason why futures combined with stop-loss orders may not be as effective as buying an option is that when the market moves against you and sets off your stop-loss order on the future, your position will be automatically sold and you are out of the market. If the market then changes directions and moves in your favor you will miss out on the profit. However, if you own a call or a put, you can just wait out a market move against you and hold onto your option until it expires. There is nothing worse in the futures than to get stopped out just $0.15 before the market changes. You got out at almost the low of the day, giving you a sizable loss, whereas if only you had stayed in you would have ended up with a nice profit.

So options do offer very important advantages over futures. Whether you believe that they are enough to outweigh the higher premiums and the other expenses will be determined by your own financial situation and your expectations of the market.

RULES OF STRATEGY IN OPTIONS

If you want to try your hand at options, here are some rules of strategy you should find helpful.

1. *Avoid far-out-of-the-money options.* Don't buy an option which is far out of the money. As we saw in our previous analysis, options are highly speculative. Unfortunately, it is not until you have lost a substantial amount of money with options that you will appreciate just how speculative they are. The purpose of this rule is to make you face the reality: Options are extremely volatile, and buying an out-of-the-money option just adds another layer of risk to an already risky venture. It is as if you decided you wanted to duplicate the feat of walking on a tightwire strung between the two World Trade Center towers in downtown Manhattan, but to make it a little more interesting, you decided to blindfold yourself.

Let's go through the figures again. In the first place, despite our pride in being able to forecast just how the market is going to be able to move, there is really a 50% chance that it will move in the other direction. That leaves you with a 50% chance to make a profit. But of the 50% chance that it will move in your favor, there is about a 5% chance that the move will be so slight as to be meaningless. That leaves a 45% chance that it will go up. But you have to pay a premium for the call, which reduces your chances considerably, perhaps to 33%. Then when you use an option with an out-of-the-money strike price, you are going to make money only on that rare, dramatic move which happens once or twice a year. And even if it does happen twice a year, that doesn't mean it will actually take place from start to finish while your option is still in existence. For example, the move might start with about one week to go, and almost reach your strike price upon the option's expiration period, and then continue on up after your option has expired, all of which will do you no good at all. Or the move might start just after you have bought your call. Let's say you buy the 170 call when the index is at 160. The index moves up dramatically to 170, then goes on up to 175. At this point you might have a modest profit, but you certainly aren't going to sell, because a lot of the premium went out of the option, and if you wait just a little bit longer, you know that you will make a much bigger profit. If you paid 4 for that 170, and the index went up to 170, the call price might just have gone to 6½ or 7. But now that the option is on the money instead of out of the money, you know that every point from now on will produce an increase in the price of the call of close to a point. So you're holding on for that additional increase. Unfortunately, what can all too easily happen now is that the market stops rising and eases off just a bit—say, to 165. Your option falls back, all the way to 4. Since this is just what you paid for it even though the market is up 5 points, you certainly are not going to sell here. You wait and so does the market, with the result that your option could easily expire worthless.

Furthermore, sometimes the point at which you will make a bigger-percentage return with an out-of-the-money option as compared with an on-the-money option, or one just slightly out of the money, is so high that it just doesn't justify the risk of losing all your money. If the 160 option is 5 and the 170 option is 2½, remember that if the index goes to 170 at the options' expiration, you will have a 100% profit in the 160 option and a 100% loss in the 170. Think about that. At 165 you break even with the 165 option while not even coming close to getting any money at all for your 170 call. But, you may reply, the big payoff comes on the upside, where my 170 option will be doubling every 2½ points. Yes. This means that if the index gets up to 175 upon expiration, you will have a profit of 100% on your option. What would you make if you had bought the 160? At 175, the 160 option is worth 15 points, and you paid 5 for it, so you would have a profit of 10, which is a 200% profit. Therefore, at 175 you are making twice as much profit from the 160 as the 170. And remember, at any price below that all the way down to 161, you are doing far, far better with the 160 call. In fact, it is not until the index gets up to 180 that you make as big a percentage profit with the 170 as with the 160. At that point the 170 is worth 10, which is a profit of 7½, which is a 300% profit; and the 160 is worth 20, which is a profit of 15 and is a 300% profit. So we find that just to make as big a percentage profit on your 170 call the index must go up by a full 20 points. What was the last time the index went up by that much in a limited time? Twenty points on the S&P 500 or VLCA indexes are equivalent to about 140 points on the Dow Jones Industrial Average. That may happen once every two years or so. And if it has happened recently, it may be even less likely that it is going to happen again soon. But remember that the chances of the index not going up to 170 are extremely good, which means that you would lose your entire stake.

The conclusion is that you don't have to pyramid risk on top of risk by buying an out-of-the-money option. If you want to play the lottery there are a lot of other places where you can do it and get the results quicker than here. Check your local newsstand for details. An on-the-money or slightly out-of-the-money option is risky enough, and the market doesn't have to move up by a near record-breaking amount for you to break even or perhaps actually make a decent profit.

2. *Deep-in-the-money options.* Think carefully before buying a deep-in-the-money option. This rule is not telling you not to buy a deep-in-the-money option but simply to be aware of the potential loss you are taking on by purchasing a deep-in-the-money put or call. First, the advantage of a deep-in-the-money put or call is that the premium you pay is a lot less than with an on-the-money or slightly out-of-the-money option. Look at these typical call prices. If the index is at 200, the 180 call may be 21, the 190 at 12, the 200 at 5 and the 210 at 2½. This means that the future time premium you are paying for the 180 call is only 1, for the 190 it is 2 and for the 200 it is 5. Whether the market goes up or down, the money you pay for the future time premium is a cost you must bear, because even if you make money in the end, it will be in spite of the fact that you are losing the entire amount of the future time value of the call, providing you hold it until maturity. So there is a temptation to buy the 180 call and save on the amount of the future time premium. That is a valid reason for buying it.

But keep in mind that you are paying a cost in other ways for reducing your premium cost. The first is the obvious one, that you must put up more money, on which you receive no interest. This is relatively minor. The second reason is far more important, however: You have a much greater amount of capital at risk for each call you buy. Remember that markets can move against you just as rapidly and as far as they move for you. When you buy a slightly out-of-the-money call, you might suspect that you will lose your entire cost. But somehow when you buy a deep-in-the-money call, you really don't expect the market to go down so far that you will lose your entire cost. But it can and often does happen. If you have been a professional on Wall Street long enough, you realize that if something can happen, and you leave yourself open to that possibility often enough, it is only a matter of time until it actually does happen. If you make a practice of buying deep-in-the-money puts or calls, one can predict with almost certainty that eventually you will lose all the money you put into one of your options. Since one of the major attractions of buying options is that it limits the amount at risk, the deep-in-the-money, expensive option eliminates one of the major reasons for buying options in the first place.

The deeper in the money the option is, the more like going long or short a future it becomes. If you find an option 30 points in the money, then for all intents and purposes a purchase of that option is just like taking a position in the futures, except that you are paying cash for the price of the option, whereas the futures buyer or seller simply puts up the required amount of margin. What this means is that depending upon the margin requirement of the futures, you might actually have to put up more money to trade the option than the futures. And like the futures trader, you would be subject to very large losses if the market moved against you. If you do decide to purchase an option under these circumstances, I suggest you use much the same trading techniques as were recommended with the futures —that is, protect yourself from large losses by using stop-loss orders where possible, or just have an informal arrangement with your broker that he will call you if it gets down to a point where you would want to get out.

3. *Various option maturities.* Before buying an option, carefully compare all the different expiration dates. As we mentioned above, one of the big differences between futures and options is the way in which the time remaining in their lives affects the price. With the futures, the price differences are relatively minor, typically increasing about a point or more for every additional three months. Any time you want to extend your future for three more months, you simply sell the one you have, buy out the next one and pay the difference. So in our discussion of futures we didn't pay very much attention to which expiration date to pick. But the pricing of options is distinctly different. The near-term option could be ¼, and the next

one could be 4; so it isn't just a matter of procedure, but a vital question which goes to the very substance of what you are doing.

The first general rule is that the longer the time remaining in the option, the higher will be the price. The next rule is that only that portion of the option's price changes that represents its future time value. Thus, if an index is at 155 and you are considering which 150 call to buy, 5 points of the option's price represents the fact that the index is already 5 points over the strike price. These 5 points are called the cash value or the intrinsic value of the call, and it is the same for the one-week option as it is for the nine-month option. It is only the rest of the option's price, which we call the time premium or the future time value, which changes. In general, there will be larger variations in the prices of out-of-the-money options than for on-the-money options, and the prices of in-the-money options will vary the least of all. Thus, with the index at 155, the 160 calls for the nearest term, if they have only a week to go, may be ¼, the next may be 2 and the next 4. The 150 calls might be priced at 5½, 7 and 8. Note that whereas the longest out-of-the-money option is priced at 16 times the shortest term, the longest in-the-money option is only 45% higher. This is primarily due to the fact that there is no change in the intrinsic part of the price and also because even the future value of an in-the-money option does not change very much.

For those with a mathematical bent, the formula for determining the theoretical time value of an on-the-money option uses the square root of the amount of time. Thus if you have one option with four weeks to go and another with sixteen weeks to go, the way to get the correct theoretical relationships is to compare the square roots. The square root of 4 is 2 and the square root of 16 is 4, so the relationship is 2 to 4, or 1 to 2, which means that the sixteen-week option should be selling at twice the price of the four-week option. Without this formula you probably would conclude that the sixteen-week option, being four times as long as the four-week option, should be worth four times as much. Not true.

In addition to being able to determine the correct theoretical relationships, you should also apply a few practical tests. The first is to ask how much you are paying per week for the option. The purchase of an option can be analogized to renting the right to make money from a change in the price of the index. And when you rent something, you naturally look at your rent in terms of units of time. So instead of asking what the price of an option is, why not ask what the cost per week of that option is? When you determine these costs for the different expiration dates, you will then have a reasonable basis for comparison.

Generally, the longer-term options will be cheaper in the per-week test. But there are offsetting considerations: You are risking more cash, and the probability of future movement of a stock is not directly proportional to the time involved. Thus, if a stock index has a historically proven variation of about 1% a day, this does not mean that thirty business days from now it is very likely to be either up or down by 30%. This is, of course, due to the fact that many of the daily changes cancel out one another, so that at the end of the month it could be only 5% or less above or below where it was yesterday.

Nevertheless, the professional trader is more likely to buy the longer-term option, and the less sophisticated members of the public are likely to go for the short-term option. In times of rapidly moving markets, the short-term options become the most overpriced. Thus if the market is moving up rapidly, it will usually be the shortest-term out-of-the-money calls which will be the most overpriced. At times like that you should seriously consider buying the longer-term options.

4. *Annualizing the option's cost.* Annualize the cost of the call to appreciate its cost. One of the tricky aspects of calls and puts is that they always look so cheap. There they are, only costing a few dollars, and we all know that the market can so easily go up or down by 25 points on the Dow Jones in one day. So imagine, if the market moved that way for just two days in a row, that call or put would more than double in just those two days. Ah, yes. The joys of dreaming. And of course this is the lure of options. Risk very little and get the possibility of making a huge amount of money. The one factor left out is this: What are the odds of making that great amount of money? After all, a state lottery offers the same opportunity, but most of us are knowledgeable enough to realize that if half the cost of the schools in our state are paid for from the lottery, then the poor saps buying those lottery tickets are not getting a very good deal, and taken on the whole, the players are not getting back nearly as much as they put in. Much the same things can happen with calls and puts. Occasionally the market will move dramatically and all the call (or the put) buyers will make a lot of money. But most of the time they lose. And one way you can prevent yourself from becoming

too much of a loser is to think of your cost of the option in annual terms.

Now, of course, we know you are not buying a one-year option but only one for four weeks, for example. Nevertheless, as we mentioned above, if you think you are renting the right to buy or sell the index at a profit, you will have a greater appreciation of what you are paying if you look at the annual rent. Thus, if you are paying $2 for an out-of-the-money call which has a month to go, multiply that by 12 to find out what you are paying on an annualized basis. Would you pay $24 for a one-year call? More dramatically, perhaps, you are buying a one-week call for just $1. Would you even consider paying $52 for a one-year call? While the comparison is not mathematically equivalent, realize that if you could buy this same call for $1 every week you would have paid $52 at the end of a year. The purpose of this calculation is to make you appreciate that a low-cost, short-term option may actually be quite expensive in terms of real value. For you it is only a one-week fling, but remember that on the other side of the transaction is a seller who has probably very carefully figured out the odds and the annualized rate of return he is getting. If he is a professional investor and has decided that most likely he is going to profit handsomely from this transaction, where does that leave you? This too is a sum-zero game. If he wins, it will only be because you lose.

5. *When your option doubles.* Sell half your calls when they double in price. One of the big problems in trading index options is that you never know when to get out. And this is a very real problem. Because when things are going your way, it *always* seems as if they will continue that way. If you have not had experience trading options or stocks, you will just have to take my word for it. But there is perhaps no more exhilarating experience than to have purchased a good number of puts and then see the market begin to crash. As the market continues to move down, you begin to count all your profits, which can become very large very quickly. The problem is that no matter how much you have made, it always seems as if the market still has farther to go. Just another 20 points and you will get out. Or just one more really good day and you'll take your profit. But when that one day more comes, you have to ask yourself, Why should I get out when the market is still moving in my direction? It is often impossible to answer that question. And you will always find plenty

of investment advisors who will say that the market is going at least 50 or 100 points lower. So you stay in. And sure enough, just when you thought it wouldn't happen, the market suddenly moves with unprecedented strength in the opposite direction. You stumble back, reeling from the shock, to count your profits, and find that they have almost disappeared. Oh well, this is clearly a one-day aberration, and you decide to hang in there until you can regain most of your vanished profits. But the market may never get back to where it was.

To overcome this problem, I strongly urge you to adopt the rule of always selling half your position when the price of your option doubles. The money you thus receive will equal your entire cost of putting on the position. You will have received back all your money and still have half the options you started with. You literally cannot lose. If the market keeps going in your direction, you have half the options you had, which will make more money for you. If the market turns against you, you already have gotten back your original cost. No matter how low your option goes, you cannot lose money, and if you sell your remaining options for anything at all, that will be your profit on the transaction.

An even greater advantage is psychological. Once you have sold half the position you can relax, knowing that what you still have at risk in the market is someone else's money. Let the options move without having to worry about sustaining a loss. Furthermore, there is a logical reason for following this rule: You automatically retain the size of your original risk. Thus, if you originally decided you would risk $2,500 on an option, and it has doubled, you now have $5,000 at risk, which is twice as much as you originally wanted. No wonder you feel a bit anxious about it. By selling half your options, you return the amount of money at risk to the original level, which should make you more comfortable.

It must be admitted that there is no mathematical reason why this rule works. In about half the cases where you sell half your position, you would have been better off not selling any at all, and in about another half of the cases it would have been best to sell out the entire position. But since in the real world we are not blessed with the gift of foresight (as we are with hindsight), this rule provides a clear course of action which will work to your benefit over the long run. But please apply it systematically. The one time you think the options are going to continue to increase could be the time they promptly return to zero.

6. Limiting original amount at risk. Never risk more than you can afford to lose comfortably. This rule should really come first; you must consider it before you do anything else. It needs very little elaboration. The simple truth is that the direction of the stock market in the near-term future is impossible to predict and that purchasing a put or a call is like a bet about which way the market is going to go in the near future. Thus, it should be obvious that there is a very good chance you will lose all the money which goes into buying either a put or a call. So don't take out a mortgage, or dip into the funds you were going to use for your daughter's tuition.

The worst thing you can do is try to get even. Let's say you bought a 160 strike price call believing that the index would move up this high. Instead, the index went down to 140. You now decide that if the market was due for a rise at its former level, it is now really ready for one, so you buy an even bigger amount of calls now to make up for the previous loss. Unfortunately, the fact that the market was higher a few weeks ago does not guarantee it is going to move up now. The market is fully capable of moving down month after month after month. The reverse is just as true. If you have bought puts, you could be waiting for years before it goes down. More often than not only after everyone, including you, decides that there really is no reason why the market should ever change direction and go up (or down), and gets out completely, does the market explode in the other direction.

Conclusion: Only speculate with small amounts you can afford to lose. If you do lose, you won't feel compelled to take risks with money you really can't afford to lose in order to get even.

CHAPTER 6
Selling Options

In the preceding chapter we discussed how you could make money by trading options—buying either a put or a call and then selling it at hopefully a higher price. And as we noted early in the chapter, options are not issued or sold by the named corporation nor by the options or futures exchanges. They are issued or sold by people like you or me because they believe they can make money by selling them. And while there are no extensive statistics yet on index options, the figures on options for individual stocks suggest that over the past ten years at least, usually the sellers of options have made the money. In this chapter we will outline just what it means to be a seller of an option on an index and will give suggestions for making those sales profitable.

Not for Everyone. First let me emphasize that selling options is clearly not for everyone. When you buy an option the worst that can happen is that you lose the money you originally committed. While this may be regrettable, it is so easy to grasp that no one should be surprised if in fact he does lose all the money he put up. But selling options is far more complex. There are two basic methods of selling options, and with both of them the risks are theoretically almost unlimited. No matter which system you use, the one fact of selling options is that the potential profit is absolutely limited, whereas the loss may be very great. Thus the sale of options should be undertaken only by people who can appreciate that even with this basic apparent disadvantage it is possible to make money under these conditions if limited profits are made much more often than large losses are taken.

The mechanics of selling options are fairly simple. You simply notify your broker that you wish to sell whichever put or call you desire. He sells it for your account. You are now short that option. This means that you are obligated to buy it back, or to accept an assignment of the underlying index, unless the option expires worthless.

WAYS TO TERMINATE YOUR POSITION

Buying back the option is easy. Let's say you sell a December 160 call for $5, which multiplied by $500 brings you $2,500. The first thing to note is that the $2,500 you receive is your money, and you are free to do anything you wish with it, including applying it as margin against any of your positions, or taking it out of your brokerage account entirely. If the index goes down and the price of that call decreases to $2, you can decide to buy it back, which would close out your position. You buy it in for 2 times $500, or $1,000. Now that you have bought it in, you no longer have a position in the option. You are out, and since you originally sold the option for $2,500, you have a profit of $1,500.

Another way to terminate a position of being short an option is to have it assigned. This means that the owner of the option has decided to exercise it—that is, to buy the underlying index or future for the price of the strike price in the case of a call, or to sell it to you in the case of a put. In this case you sold a call with a 160 strike price. If a holder of a call similar to the one you sold decided to exercise it, he will pay $160 times 500, or $80,000, to acquire the underlying index or futures contract. From your point of view, this means that you will have to accommodate the option buyer. If you sold a call at the 160 strike price, you must be willing to deliver out the underlying index or future for a price of 160, or $80,000.

Here is where a big distinction comes in between an option on an index, like the CBOE-100, and an option on a futures contract like the S&P 500. In the assignment of an option on a futures contract there is actual transfer or delivery of the futures contract, so that if you were assigned on a call option on a futures which you had sold, in an assignment you would sell one contract for the exercise price of the call. In the case of an option on an index, there is simply an entry made for the amount of money represented by the index. When an option on a futures contract is assigned on the last day of the future's life, there is also no transfer of any contract, since the future is expiring, but there is simply a money adjustment.

If you had sold a put rather than a call originally, then if you were assigned it would mean that the person on the other side who bought the put had decided to exercise his put and sell to you for the strike price, the underlying index or future. Thus, when you are assigned on your put, you will be buying the index for the strike price. If you sold a 160 put, then you will have to pay out 160 times $500, or $80,000, and you will be credited with the current price of the index.

A third method of terminating being short an option is for the option to expire. This will happen only if the option is out of the money on the expiration date. For example, if you are short a call at, say, the 140 strike price, and the index is at 138, then the call would be worthless and there would be no purpose served for the option owner if he were to exercise it. So he will simply let it expire, and you will have completed your transaction; in this case, the entire price for which you sold the option in the first place becomes your profit on the transaction. Incidentally, if you are short an option you have no control over whether or when it is assigned.

We will now turn to a more detailed discussion of the two basic ways to sell options. One is to sell covered options, in which case you are long a future for every call option you sell, and short a future for every put you sell; the other method involves selling calls and puts without having any position in the underlying index.

WRITING COVERED CALLS

Covered call writing consists of buying a future and selling a call option on it with the same or shorter expiration period: Technically, you are long the future and short the call. The objective of this strategy is to take advantage of the fact that the future time value of the call option is usually much greater than the premium which the stock-index future carries over its underlying index. For example, let's assume that one of the indexes is at 140. The June future is at 141 with about three months to go. This is a 1-point premium over the index. But the June 140 strike-price option is selling at 5. Thus it has a future time value of 5. Your objective is to buy the stock-index future with its 1-point premium, sell the option with its 5-point premium and hopefully make a profit of 4 points, which would of course be $2,000 per option.

Covered Option Example. Let's see how this would work. You buy the future and sell the option. Let's assume that at the option's expiration date the index is at 140. With the index right at the strike price, the option is not likely to be exercised, since its owner could just as easily purchase the index on the futures exchange for the same price as his strike price. So we will assume that the option expires unexercised, and you sell your futures contract for 140. Since you bought your contract at 141 you have a loss of 1 point, or $500. The option also is expiring worthless, and since you sold it for $5, you now have a profit in it of 5 times $500, or $2,500. Subtracting your loss in the futures contract from your gain in the option gives you your profit of $2,000. This is obviously a contrived situation, since the index is not very likely to go out right at the strike price, so let's see what happens when the index is up or down.

We will use the same facts, where you buy the June future at 141 and sell the June 140 call at 5. Now let's assume the index moves up to 150 at expiration, again assuming that you have not been assigned the call before the final date. If you do nothing, then on the final date the call will be assigned, which means you are selling the index for 140 times $500, or $70,000. The exercise of the call is also its termination, so the call disappears from your account. This means that you are left with $70,000. You originally bought the June contract for 141 or $70,500, which means you have a loss of $500 on the futures contract. But remember that you sold the option for 5, or $2,500. Since the option has now vanished, you have that profit to offset against your loss on the future, which means that you have achieved your goal of making a profit of 4 points, or $2,000.

In this example it doesn't matter how high the index goes; the results are always the same. Whether it goes up to 141 or 181, the call will be exercised. This means that you will sell the index for 140. It is totally irrelevant to you how high the index is. You must sell it for 140, and this means you will make your profit of 4 points per option. You are limiting your profit on the upside to the 4-point difference between the future time value of the option and the premium you paid for the futures contract.

So you make $2,000 per contract if the index stays right at the strike price or goes up by any amount. But what happens if the index goes down? Assume that it falls from 140 to 130 at expiration date. Since the owner of the call option can buy the index on the futures exchange for approximately 130, he is not interested in buying it from you for 140 by exercising his call. So he declines, and the option expires. You are now left owning the futures contract, which will also expire, and therefore you will be treated as if you sold it on the final day, leaving you with a loss of 11 points times $500, or $5,500, on the futures contract. Your original sale of the option for 5 brought in $2,500, and with the expiration of the call, this amount becomes your profit from the sale of the call. Therefore you subtract the $2,500 profit from the call from the $5,500 loss on the futures to give you your overall loss of $3,000.

As you can see, the basic principle here is that when the futures decline, you can offset the loss on the futures by the amount of money you took in from the sale of the option. If the index declines to just 139, then you suffered a 2-point loss in the futures contract, or $1,000, but you received $2,500 from the sale of the call, so you actually made a profit of the difference between those two of $1,500. To summarize if the index closes at 140 or higher, you will make a profit of 4 points, or $2,000, and if it closes lower than 140, you will take the loss on the futures and subtract $2,500 from that loss to get your results. This means that the break-even point for you will be 136 on the index. If the index closes above that point you will make money; if it closes below that point you will lose money.

From this example you can already see that one reason for selling covered calls is that it takes a limited amount of risk out of owning a futures contract. Here you are fully protected against any loss if the index drops by up to 4 points. And if it stays still or goes up, you will make a very reasonable profit. Thus covered call writing is for the person trying to make a good return on his money but not attempting to make a big killing. It also means that the odds favor making some money. Remember, the covered call writer makes money if the market goes up, stays still or goes down by less than the amount covered by his call. This means that only in the case of a major decline in the market will he lose money; therefore, the probability is that most of the time the covered call writer will make money.

Two variations of covered call writing are important to consider. The example we just looked at was an on-the-money call. Covered call writing with out-of-the-money and deep-in-the-money options also has special advantages. If a person is basically optimistic on the market but would like to have a small hedge in case he is wrong, he should consider selling an out-of-the-money call. On the other hand, if a person wants to be defensive and is worried that the market might come down, he should consider writing a deep-in-the-money call. I hope it goes without saying that since covered call writing by its very nature provides only a limited hedge against a downturn in the market, a pessimist on the market should not write even deep-in-the-money calls.

OUT-OF-THE-MONEY CALLS

First let's examine writing out-of-the-money calls for a person who believes the market will go up. If he were certain that the market would really go up dramatically in the near future, then he would not write any calls. But this person has a healthy skepticism about his own ability to forecast, and he would be quite happy with a good-percentage appreciation without breaking the bank. He likes the idea of taking in money from selling calls, so that if the market doesn't go up he will still make money. For this person, selling out-of-the-money calls makes a lot of sense.

Let us return to our original example, where the index was at 140 and the June contract was 141 and the June 140 call option was 5. At that same time there was a June 150 strike-price call at 3 and a 160 call at 1½. Our trader decides that he will sell the 150 option for 3. So he buys the June futures contract for 141 and sells the June 150 option for 3. This means that he has taken in 3 times $500, or $1,500, for the option. Now let's see what happens at the expiration. There are once again two major possibilities. First, if the contract is below 150, the option will not be exercised. This means that our trader keeps the entire $1,500 he took in from the sale of the option as his profit from the sale. Whether the overall transaction results in a profit depends upon how much he makes or loses on the futures contract. If the contract stays at 140, then he has a loss of 1 point, or $500 in the futures. This means that his net profit on the transaction is $1,000 less all transaction costs.

If the contract has fallen, then his loss on the futures has to be subtracted from the $1,500 profit on the option to give his net return. Note that in this example he will make money if the contract is above 139.50, whereas in the first example his break-even point was 136. Since the price of an out-of-the-money option is always less, and substantially less than the price of an on-the-money option, you will always have less downside protection from an out-of-the money option, and your break-even point will always be higher. Below 139.50, the loss is point for point for each additional point lower on the contract price. But no matter how low the contract goes, the person in our example is always $1,500 ahead of a person who did not sell the option.

Now let's look at the upside. You recall that in our example of the on-the-money call, it did not matter how high the contract closed, because it would be called away at 140 if it closed at any price above that amount. Here is the major difference with the out-of-the-money option. Since the strike price of this option is 150, it does make a difference how high the contract closes, because the writer of the 150 option gets to keep all the profit in the contract for any price up to 150. Thus, if the contract closes at 146, it is still below the 150 strike price so the option will not be assigned. Therefore the option expires worthless and the person in our example can sell the futures contract for 146. Since he paid 141 for it, he has a profit on the futures of 5 points, which is $2,500. He also has the profit of $1,500 in the option, so that his total profit on the transaction is $4,000. Note that this is $1,500 higher than if he had not sold the option, and $2,000 higher than if he had sold the on-the-money option. In fact, at any price of the contract above 141, the writer of the 150 option makes money two ways, first from the money he took in from the sale of the option, and second from the full profit in the price appreciation of the contract.

This is the big attraction of writing out-of-the-money options. For at least a certain price range, you can have your cake and eat it too, that is, take in money from sale of the option and make the full profit on the futures contract. At prices above 150, the profit freezes. In this case, the profit would be the $1,500 from the option, plus the 9 point rise in the contract, which is $4,500, for a total profit of $6,000. This is as high as the profit can get, because at all prices above 150 the contract will be called away for 150. Thus you can summarize the appeal of writing out-of-the-money calls by stating that you get a significant amount of money from selling the call (although admittedly much less than from selling an on-the-money call) and are entitled to a substantial profit if the futures contract rises.

IN-THE-MONEY CALLS

In-the-money call selling is just the reverse. It gives significantly greater protection in case the contract declines, but the potential profit is less than with an on-the-money contract. In this case, where the futures contract was at 141, the June 130 contract was at 12. As soon as a person sells that 130 strike-price contract, he has promised to sell the index for 130. This means that since he bought it for 141, he has an automatic 11-point loss in the contract the minute he sells the option. That's the bad news. The good news is that he sold the call for 12, and if the contract is called away—that is, if the option is assigned—he will have a profit of 12 from the option. So this means there is a net profit on the transaction of 1, or $500 per contract. That is the net profit, provided the contract does not close below 130. This is a shorthand way of saying that if the contract is anywhere above 130 when the option expires, the option will be exercised, and the contract will be called away at 130, so that at any point above 130 there will be a profit of 1 point. At 130 there is that profit of 1 point, which means that the break-even point in this transaction is 129. For every point that the contract closes below 129 at the expiration date, there will be a loss of 1 more point.

In summary, by selling a deep-in-the-money call like this 130 call, the investor has reduced his break-even point dramatically—from 141 in the case of the person who does not sell a call, down to 129. This means that by selling an in-the-money call, a person can give himself 12 points of downside protection. One would not usually see an index move down by more than that in any three-month period. The negative is that the potential profit is frozen at a relatively modest level—in this case, just 1 point. So you are converting a very risky venture—going long a stock-index-futures contract—into something which is not quite so risky, because you will make a profit unless the contract plummets by more than 12 points; and you are removing the opportunity to make anything more than a modest profit.

UNCOVERED OPTION SELLING

The other basic type of option selling is to sell options when you do not have an offsetting position in the futures. This is called uncovered or naked option selling. It is considered quite risky because, at least in the case of uncovered call writing, there is a virtually unlimited risk if the index suddenly takes off, and in the case of uncovered put selling the risk is almost as great because the index can plummet just about as far down as it can go up. Let's take the same example we used before, where the index was 140, the June futures contract was 141, the June 140 call was 5 and the June 150 call was 3. If a person believes that the market is not going to go up in the near future, he might decide to sell the June 140 call. He does so, and as we said before, the money he takes in—the $2,500 per option—is his to keep. Of course, he must put up the required amount of margin for selling an uncovered call. (See the margin section for a discussion of the amount.) At this point our speculator is short one June 140 option. If, at the expiration of the option, the contract is 140 or anywhere below that, the option will not be exercised. It will expire worthless, and the seller will keep the entire proceeds of $2,500 as his profit. Note that he keeps all ties. That is, if the index goes down or stays right where it is, he keeps the entire amount of the option.

If the contract closes above 140, the option will be assigned. This means that his account will be debited for the amount the index is above 140. Thus, for every point that the index is above 140, he will be charged an additional $500. For example, if the index is at 145, then he is behind by 5 points, or $2,500. Remember, however, that he originally sold his call for 5 points, or $2,500, so that in this example he is actually breaking even when the index goes up by 5 points. Therefore we can see that his break-even point is equal to what he took in from the option added onto the strike price.

Thus not only does an uncovered call writer keep all ties, he also breaks even when the market moves against him, in this case by 5 points in the index. At any point between the strike price and this break-even point he makes money—that is, at any point in our example between 140 and 145. If the index closes at 143 at the call's expiration, the option will be assigned. This means that he will be charged the difference between the strike price of his call, 140, and the price of the index, 143. Thus he will lose 3 points on the index, but he took in 5 points from the original sale of the option, so he has the difference of 2 points as his profit. At any price of the index at expiration above 145 he will lose point for point. For example, if the index closes at 150 upon the option's expiration, he will be assigned on his option and will suffer a loss of 10 points on the contract, offset by his 5 original points from the option, giving him a loss of 5 points on the transaction. That is why selling uncovered calls can be so dangerous. If the market decides to stage a major rally just after you have sold some calls, you could have an enormous loss when your option is assigned.

In these examples, we have assumed that the option was not assigned until its expiration and that the writer of the option did nothing. This was to explain the mechanics. In real life, the writer of a call would undoubtedly buy back the call before he got involved in the big losses he could face if he waits to have his option assigned. It should be emphasized that selling options is a completely liquid transaction—it can be closed out at any time simply by buying in the options which were originally sold. So while it may be risky, at least under normal circumstances when there are no big gap moves, there is no chance of being trapped into a situation you can not get out of.

OUT-OF-THE-MONEY UNCOVERED OPTIONS

Now that we have seen how selling an uncovered call works, we can look at the two variations of it: selling-out-of-the-money and in-the-money calls. In fact, sale of out-of-the-money calls will probably become the most popular form of naked call selling. Selling an out-of-the-money call uncovered is just like selling an out-of-the-money covered call except that you do not have a position in the underlying index. So, in our example, you might decide to sell the 150 June call for 3 when the index was at 140. This means you have taken in the 3 points, $1,500, and it will be yours to keep unless at the expiration of the call the index is at 150 or higher. If the index is above 150, of course, the option will be assigned, and for every point it is above 150, you will lose an additional point on assignment. Thus, since you initially took in 3 points, your break-even point is at 153. Below that you make money, and above that you lose point for point.

But let's look at the situation once you have sold the 150 call. First of all, the index has a roughly 50% chance of going down. Great. You pick up the $1,500 you took without any sweat. There is some chance it will stay right around the 140 point. Terrific. Same as above. Then there is also the 50% chance that the index will go up. But by how much? Studies of stock market price predictions indicate that there is the greatest probability that the market will end up in the same general area it started from and that for every point above or below the starting number there is a rapidly decreasing probability that it will reach that point. This is known as the bell-curve effect. See Figure 5. Since the greatest probability is that it will not stray far from where it started, and you will lose money on your out-of-the-money call only if the market does move significantly up, the odds are very good that you will win. Selling out-of-the-money uncovered calls is one of the few speculations you can get into where you can win even when you are a bit wrong on the market. You don't sell uncovered calls unless you believe the market is going to stay about where it is, or go down. But if it goes up, you can still make your full profit as long as it doesn't go above your strike price.

IN-THE-MONEY UNCOVERED CALLS

The other variation of uncovered call writing is to sell in-the-money

Probability of Price Swings

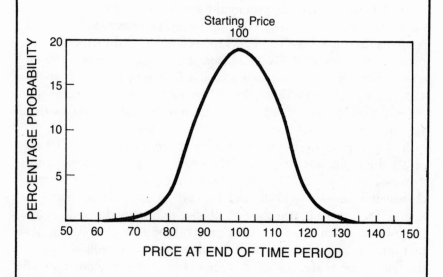

Figure 5

calls. In our example where the index was 140, you might decide to sell the 130 call for 12. You would do this if you believe the market is going to go down, but you don't want to lose money if you are wrong and it doesn't go down but stays where it is. You want the market to move down below 130 on the expiration date of the call. In that case the call expires unassigned, and you pick up the entire 12 points, or $6,000 per option. If the index stays where it is at 140, you would be assigned at the strike price of your call, 130, and have a loss of 10. But you received 12 for the call, so you have a profit of 2 on the transaction. Thus your break-even point is 142, and for every point above that you would have a loss of 1 more point. For every point below 142 you make a point profit until you reach 130, where you make the maximum of 12 points.

Selling uncovered in-the-money calls thus has less profit potential if the index stays still than selling the on-the-money call, and it will have much greater losses than selling out-of-the-money calls if the index moves up against you, but it will make a far greater profit if the index moves down, as you hope.

SELLING UNCOVERED PUTS

Now we will discuss the other half of selling uncovered options, which is selling puts. As you will recall, a put buyer has the right to sell the index at a fixed price. When you sell a put, you are obligating yourself to buy in the index at a fixed price. If the index falls below the strike price of your put, then it will be assigned, and you will have to pay for the amount below the strike price of your put. For example, if the index had been 140, when you sold the June 140 put for 4, and the index then went down to 130 at the put's expiration, your put would be assigned. In theory this means that you would buy in the index at 140, and since it was only worth 130, you would then sell it out for that price, showing a loss of 10 on the index. In reality, of course, there is no buying and selling, and your account is just debited the 10 points. But you took in 5 points from selling the put originally, so your total loss was only 5 points. If the index was at 140 or higher on the expiration date of the put, the owner of the put would have no reason to sell it to you for less than the current price. Your option would therefore expire unexercised.

From this we can see that the person who sells puts basically does not believe the market will go down. He knows that his potential profit is limited to the amount of money he originally receives from the sale of the put, and he recognizes that if the market declines precipitously, he could face very large losses. But he sells puts because the odds are in his favor. Once again, he will make money if the market stays just where it is, and he will only lose money if it moves against him by enough to equal the amount he took in from the sale of the put. In this case, where he sold the 140 put for 4, his break-even point would be 136. Below that point he would lose point for point. Between 136 and 140 he would make a profit, starting with a zero profit at 136 and going up point for point with the index until he reached his maximum profit of 4 at 140. Above 140 he would continue to make his maximum profit of 4.

SELLING IN- AND OUT-OF-THE-MONEY PUTS

Uncovered put selling can also be divided into three different forms. There is the on-the-money put, which we have just discussed. There is also the out-of-the-money put and the in-the-money put. The seller of an out-of-the-money put sells a put with a strike price below the current price of the index. In this way he has a greater chance of the index not going below his strike price and therefore a greater chance of ending up with the entire proceeds of the put as his profit. The negative consideration is that the price he receives for the put is less than the one for the on-the-money put or for an in-the-money put, so his potential profit is substantially less.

The sale of the in-the-money put has a strike price above the current price of the index. For instance, if the index is now at 140, the sale of the 150 strike-price put would be the sale of an in-the-money put. It would probably fetch a price of at least 12. This means that the maximum profit would be 12, since the full price of the put will become the profit on the transaction if the index rises above 150 and the put expires without being assigned. On the other hand, if the index goes down by just 2 points, it has reached the break-even point. Thus the sale of an in-the-money put is for someone who believes the market is going to go up. The potential profit is great if the view is correct, but there is little room for error if the market goes down instead.

MARGIN REQUIREMENTS FOR SELLING
UNCOVERED OPTIONS ON FUTURES

The purchaser of a call or put has to pay the full cash price. But what about the seller? Can he just sell the option and walk away with the

140

price he receives? When you consider the legal obligation he has placed on himself, you will understand that will hardly be the result. In fact, since the seller of an option on an index or a future is committing himself to a legal obligation, there must be some method of binding him to keep that legal obligation. On Wall Street the seller of the option must leave a certain amount of money with the brokerage firm; if the index moves against the seller, the brokerage firm will have enough funds on hand so it can close out the position and still have money left.

First we will discuss how the amount of margin is computed for someone selling a naked option on a stock-index-futures contract— that is to say, when he is not long the futures itself. The amount of margin required is equal to (1) the current price of the option (2) plus the margin on the futures contract and (3) less half the amount that the contract is out of the money, if it is out of the money. And (4) the minimum margin cannot be less than $1,000 plus the current price of the call.

Let's consider an example of this rather cumbersome statement. Suppose you sell a call with an exercise price of 150 when the future is actually 145—that is, you are selling a call 5 points out of the money. Its current price is $2,250. Going back to the rule above, the first step is to take the current price of the option, here $2,250. The second step is to add in the margin required for the futures contract. If we are talking about the S&P 500 and you are a speculator, that would be $6,000, which gives a total so far of $8,250. The third step says that we can subtract half the amount by which the option is out of the money. Since the future is now at 145 and the strike price of your option is 150, that means it is 5 points out of the money, for a cash equivalency of $500 times that for $2,500, half of that is $1,250. Subtracting that from the $8,250 gives us our margin requirement of $7,000. The fourth and final step is to check that this amount is more than the minimum, the price of the option plus $1,000, which here would be $2,250 plus $1,000, or $3,250, which is less than we arrived at. Therefore the minimum is not applicable, and the proper margin requirement is $7,000.

In computing the amount of margin you need in your account it is good to know that the money you take in from selling the option counts toward the margin requirement. As mentioned earlier, as soon as you sell an option, that money is yours to do with as you wish, and if you want to apply it toward the margin requirement, that is perfectly all right. Therefore, in the above example, where your margin requirement was $7,000, since you took in $2,250 from selling the option, you can subtract that from the requirement, giving $4,750. Therefore, if you sold the option today for $2,250, you would only have to have an additional $4,750 in your account to cover the margin requirement.

Another important point about margin is that it is marked to the market daily. This means that every day your brokerage firm's margin department will compute the margin requirements for your positions, using the closing prices from the previous day. Therefore you cannot sell an option and forget about it. Even if it is your conviction not to buy it back until the expiration date, you must realize that your margin requirement will change from day to day. And even if you do not intend to close out the position, the amount of margin may become so great that unless you have a tremendous amount of money available to meet the margin call, you might be forced to take some action to meet it.

MARGIN FOR SELLING A
COVERED CALL ON A FUTURES

In the previous section we discussed margin requirements where you sold an option naked—that is, without any position in the futures. But what would the requirement be if you are long the futures itself and then sell a futures contract against it? In such a case you might expect that the margin would be less, since if the option moves against you, the futures will automatically be moving in your favor. For instance, if you sold a 150 strike-price call and were long a futures contract at 145, then if the futures moved up to 155, you would probably have a loss on the option, but you would have a gain of 10 points on the futures. In other words, you are hedged, meaning that your exposure to loss on the option is less, and this therefore should mean that the margin requirement is also less.

Fortunately, this is one of those times where logic does coincide with reality. The margin requirement is less than for naked options. The rule is that (1) the current price of the option plus (2) the hedge margin on the futures contract (3) less half the amount by which the option is in the money. Finally, (4) there is the requirement that the margin cannot be less than the current price of the option plus $1,000. Thus the formula is identical to that for naked options, except that in the second step we use the hedge margin requirement on the futures. This makes an enormous difference when you recall that the hedge requirements on the NYSE are $1,500, compared to $3,500 for speculators; $2,500 for the S&P, vs. $6,000; and $3,250 for the VLCA, compared to $6,500.

MARGIN ON OPTIONS ON INDEXES

Figuring the amount of margin required for selling an option on an index is completely different from the method used for computing the margin required for selling an option on a future. Since an option on an index is treated like a stock option rather than a commodity, it is not surprising that its margin requirement is figured in a manner similar to selling an option on an individual stock.

The margin is figured in a three-step process, with a final fourth step to make sure that the amount is not less than a minimum requirement. The first step is to have an amount equal to the current value of the option. The second step is to add 10% of the current value of the index. The current value of the index is its price multipled by whatever multiplier is used. For example, with the CBOE-100 the multiplier is 100. The third step is to subtract the amount by which the option is out of the money. To figure the amount by which the option is out of the money you subtract the current price of the index from the exercise price of the call, then multiply by the multiplier. In the case of a put, you subtract the amount by which the exercise price of the put is below the current index price. This gives you the margin requirement. The fourth step is to check that the amount is not less than the minimum. The minimum is the current price of the option plus 2% of the price of the index, multiplied by the multiplier.

One final point to keep in mind is that on the day you sell the option, you may use the full amount you received from the sale of the option to pay for part of the margin.

A Margin Example. Let's take an example of how we might determine the amount of margin for selling a typical call. Let's say that the index we want to use is at 150 and we want to sell a call at the 155 strike price, which has a current price of $4. The multiplier of this index is $100. The first step is simply to take the value of the option, which is $4 times $100 to give us $400. The second step is to take 10% of the price of the index multiplied by the multiplier. This is 10% times 150, giving 15, times $100, which is $1,500. Thus our total requirement so far is $1,900. The third step is to subtract the amount by which the call is out of the money. Here the index is currently at 150 and we are selling a call at the 155 strike price, so it is 5 points out of the money. Multiplying this by the $100 multiplier gives us $500. We subtract this from the $1,900 we had before, giving us a margin requirement of $1,400.

The fourth step is simply to make sure that this amount is not less than the minimum. To figure the minimum we take the current price of the option, which is $4, and then add 2% of the price of the index. The index is now at 150, and 2% of it gives us $3. Adding $4 and $3 gives us $7. We multiply this by the multiplier of 100 and arrive at $700. Since the original figure of $1,400 is larger than this minimum, we can disregard it.

Thus we have calculated that the margin requirement for this position is $1,400. As we mentioned before, to compute the amount needed on the day you sell the option, you can subtract the amount you took in from its sale. So you can take $400 from this amount, which means that in order to sell a 155 strike-price call for $4 when the index is at 150, you will need to have margin available of $1,000.

PROFIT POTENTIAL OF UNCOVERED SELLING

From this calculation you can begin to see the profit potential which exists from selling uncovered puts and calls if the index does not move against you. If the index in our example does not go above 150 before the option expires, then you would have made a profit of $400 from the option on a capital requirement of $1,000, which is a 40% profit on your money. This example is based upon an actual situation involving an option which had 3½ months left. If you were able to sell a call like this three times a year and were successful each time, you would be able to make a return on your capital of over 120%.

It must be emphasized that in many cases the index will move against you so that you will have to buy in your options at a loss, or you will experience a loss on the settlement date. In other cases you may win in the end, but because the index moves against you during part of the time you are short the option, the margin requirements would be much higher, requiring substantially more capital. Like the other margin requirements described in this chapter, this requirement is marked to the market daily. This means that if you have sold a call and the index moves up, you will experience sharply increased margin requirements. Each of the three steps will be larger, and particularly the second step will result in steeply higher requirements. So when planning to sell uncovered options, you must have a substantial amount of reserve margin available.

That in a nutshell is the basic description of selling covered and uncovered options. Neither one is recommended for people who do not really want to get involved with the market by paying close attention to it on a daily basis and who are not willing to take all the risks they represent. Naked-option selling has the risk of almost unlimited losses. One problem is that people going into it understand quite well the advantage which selling uncovered options gives, that you can make money even when the market goes against you because you have the future time value (or premium) of the option as your potential profit, plus the fact that when you sell an out-of-the-money option you will make money unless the index moves far enough against you to go beyond the strike price plus the original price of the option. This tends to set up a sense of false confidence by the option seller, which can be his undoing. The same thing can happen to the seller of the covered option. He also knows he is in a hedged position and that while the profit he can make is limited, he will not lose money until the index moves against him by more than a certain amount. The problem is that these things do happen, and they seem to happen more often than the option writers ever expect they will. At least when people go long or short a futures contract, or buy a put or a call, they are under no illusions that there is any safety or protection in those positions. This tends to mean that they protect themselves more quickly against large losses. Please don't let the so-called "hedged" aspects of the positions we are discussing lull you into a sense of security and safety which simply isn't there. You may have a few points' leeway, but you still have to act as decisively as anyone to cut your losses once those few points have been reached. Therefore it is vitally important that option sellers practice these rules of strategy.

OPTION SELLERS' RULES OF STRATEGY

1. *Plan what you will do when the market moves against you.* I know that this is the same rule laid out in the chapter on trading stock-index futures. But it is even more important here, for the compelling reason that when you are a seller of options, your profits are absolutely limited. Thus, unless you are also going to limit your losses, you can readily conclude that you will lose. It takes only one loss of 25 points to

wipe out the entire profit from ten perfect sales of 2½ points each. And that represents a very realistic projection of just what can happen to someone who sells options on eleven occasions. He can be a winner for two years, and then one trade can put him in the deficit column. Selling options is like playing with dynamite. You can't trust them for a minute. Any fool will tell you that you can't make money in a situation where your gain is limited and your losses are unlimited. The truth is that you can make money provided you take all the limited gains but also limit your losses. It is relatively simple to implement a mechanical system which will limit your losses.

For the covered option seller, the way to limit losses is to place a good-till-canceled order on the future, to close out your position in the future when it goes a certain amount against you. Then as soon as you receive a report that the order has been executed, you would buy in your option at the market price at that time. For example, assume you are selling the June 140 call for 5, as in our example, when the index was 140 and you bought a June futures contract for 141. You could make a profit of 4 points, and your break-even point is 136 on the index. The question is where to put the stop-loss order on the future. If you place it at 136, so that you will sell out your futures contract if it gets down to that point, then you are out of the futures contract, and if it comes back up later you will not participate in the profit. Furthermore, you will have to buy in the June 140 call you sold, unless you are willing to convert your covered position into an uncovered one. When you do buy in the call, then whatever it costs you will have to be added onto the 5 points you lost on the futures contract, so that instead of breaking even you will sustain a loss. If you don't buy in the call, then you are in the position of being naked the call, which means that you now hope the contract will go down, whereas before, when you were covered, you were hoping it would stay up. Did you really change your view of which way the market was heading, or is this just a convenient form of wishful thinking?

If you place the stop-loss order farther down, there is less likelihood that the order will go off, and of course you hope it will not go off, because it could always come back up again and give you a profit. But if you put it too far down, then when it does go off, you will have sustained a substantial loss. If it is too high, then when it goes off you won't suffer much of a loss, but it is much more likely to go off and deprive you of the chance to make much of a profit. The actual point you choose depends upon how much profit you could make from the call and how much loss you are willing to sustain to make that profit. As a suggestion, if you had a chance to make a 5-point profit if all went well, then perhaps you would place your stop-loss order where there would be a 5-point loss. The theory behind this is that since the law of probabilities favors the contract going up or staying at about the same place, or going down slightly, the number of times when you would lose 5 points should be many fewer than the number of times when you would not.

On uncovered options, the situation is much the same. When you sell a naked put or call, you know how far the index can move against you before you will have a loss. Typically you will want to close out your position when the index reaches the strike price if you are selling out-of-the-money puts or calls. So if you sell the 150 call when the index is 140, you would buy in your call when the index gets up to 150. This may or may not produce a loss. If enough time has passed since you sold the call, and you got a high enough price for it originally, you may be able to buy back your call at the same or even a lower price than you sold it for. Usually it will cost you more. But the loss is worth it, because it is only by taking little losses that you are able to prevent yourself from having the big ones. And you can sustain a lot of little losses, because there should be enough good profit in the naked puts and calls which do work out to offset these small losses. Remember that you cannot afford one very large loss. Some people prefer to close out their positions at 1 or 2 points before the index gets to the strike price because the options are cheaper then. Others prefer to wait until the index gets 1 or 2 points beyond the strike price because then they don't have to buy in the options when the index gets just through the strike price and then turns around again. Just exactly where you decide to close out your positions is a matter of personal preference.

But there can be no question of whether to buy in your calls when they become losers. If you don't, you are playing right into the hands of the option buyers. Why don't you let them make their money from someone else? We cannot stress too much that it is imperative to close out those losers at a predetermined price. And to make sure you do it, write down just what your closeout level is, and stick to it. I can tell you from my own experience and that of many customers that closing out losers is difficult psychologically. Your emotions will be telling you to wait, that perhaps another five minutes will see the

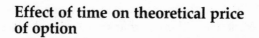

Effect of time on theoretical price of option

Chart assumes that the stock remains at the same price and the option is on the money

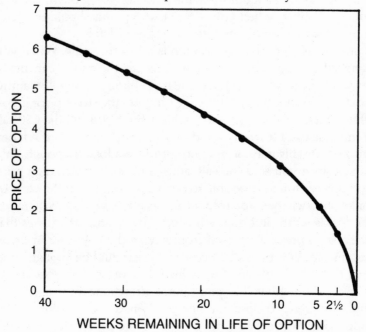

Note that in first ten weeks the option price declines $.82, whereas in the last ten weeks it loses $3.20.

Figure 6

index turn around and go back to leave you with a rich profit. Of course, that could be correct. Unfortunately, no one has come up with any other way to limit your losses. And you must limit your losses. So as soon as you put on the position, decide what you are going to do if it goes against you, write down at what price you are going to do it and then stick to what you have written down.

2. *The short-term options usually give the fastest profits.* Carefully check the prices of the various-duration options before you decide which to sell. The simplest test is simply to divide the amount of each option by the number of weeks remaining in its life to determine the amount of money you will be taking in per week. You will find that in most cases the nearest-term option has the highest return. Another advantage of the near-term option is that when it reaches its expiration date, you are automatically out of the position. If you are selling uncovered calls options the strain of hoping that the market does not go up too high can get to be a lot to bear, and you may be very pleased when your call expires. If you are selling covered calls, the strain of hoping that the index will not fall too far can also get to you, and it can be a relief that the option has expired. Another advantage to selling short-term options is that you will make your full profit potential over their duration, whereas if you have to get out of a longer-term option in less than the full term, you will not be getting your pro rata share of its price. This is because the future time value of an option does not decline in an equal amount every week. An illustration of the price decline of a typical option is shown in Figure 6.

Notice that the greatest decline comes in the final days of the option's life. Therefore you will generally receive more per unit of time from selling a short-term option. The other advantage can be explained by noting what happens if you sell a three-month option and a six-month option but then decide to close out the six-month option at the end of three months. Then it is clear that the three-month option will expire, and regardless of whether it produces a profit, at least the future time value element of its price will be zero. But with the six-month option you will probably not see the future time value of the option reduced to half, because of the way option prices work. It might very well have given up only about a third or even just a fourth of its future time value. In that case you will be making even less profit than you expected at first when you figured how much profit you were going to make per week. Thus it will usually work out better for you if instead of selling one six-month option, you sell a three-month option. When it expires you will have the choice of simply walking away from the positions or of writing another three-month option.

3. *When writing covered options, be careful not to write options far out of the money.* The purpose of writing covered calls is to take in money from the options you are writing, whether puts or calls, and to have an off-set against the movement of the index itself. If you sell far-out-of-the-money options, you are taking in so little money that it is really insignificant in relation to how far the index itself can move. This means that you are not taking in enough money to do you any good if the index moves against you. On the other hand, if it moves in your favor, you are cutting off your chance to make a really large amount of money because you are limited to the amount you can make at the strike price of the option you have sold.

For example, assume you want to write a covered call against an index currently at 147. The 150 strike-price call with three months to go is selling at 10, the 160 call is selling for 4 and the 170 call is 1½. Before we discuss which option to select let's review why you are selling covered calls. You are not doing it because you have a strong conviction on which way the market is going to go. If you thought you really knew it would be going up by a large amount in the next two months, you would not be selling a call against your long position in the index. It is easy enough simply to go long the index at 150, and when it gets to 160 or 170, sell out and make a very good profit without all the limitations and complications caused by writing a call against that position. No; the reason you are selling a call against that position is that you admit you do not know which way the market is going to go, but you doubt it will go very far down in the next two months. So you do not want to take on a long position in the contract because you don't have any conviction on which way it is going to go. In fact, you may believe it will stay within a narrow range. But if someone is willing to pay you enough, you will take a long position, because you believe that the amount they are going to pay you will probably outweigh the amount by which the index will go down. Note carefully that there is a risk in taking the long position. Obviously it could take a nose dive at any time, and you want to be compensated for taking that risk. Remember too that by selling your call you are limiting your potential profit. There is almost no limit on the loss you can take, but there is a limit on the profit you can make, so you should be handsomely compensated.

Looking at our example, we note that the 150 call is at 10, which means that if the index moves down 10 points in the next three months you would break even. On the upside, if it goes up to 150 or higher and you let the position expire, you will make the 10 points from the sale of the call plus the 3-point move from 147 to 150, for a total gain of 13. That's equal to about 8.6% of the value of the index position, which for three months means that on an annualized basis you would be earning at the rate of 34.4%, which is pretty good. The important point here is that the index may just as well go against you, and you will have only the 10 points from the sale of the option standing between you and a loss. These 10 points amount to about 6.8% of the index, which is a fairly reasonable protection for three months.

Now let's look at the situation if you sell the 160 option for 4. On the fun side, if the index goes up to 160, you will make the 13 points between the current price of the index of 147 and the option strike price of 160, plus the price of the option of 4, making a total potential profit of 17 points. This is a possible profit of about 11.5%, which is significantly better than you could have received from the 150 option. But this will happen only if the index moves up by 13 points, and you aren't at all sure this will happen. If the index moves the other way, you have only 4 points protecting you from a loss. That's just 2.7% protection, and the way the stock indexes move, that is not much protection at all. If the index starts moving down, how do you protect yourself? With a stop-loss order just 4 points below the current price? That kind of order could go off the very next day after you put on the position. In fact, both the VLCA and S&P 500 often move 4 points in one day. The point is that this isn't much of a hedge.

The sale of the 170 call is, of course, even more extreme. Here you are selling an option 23 points out of the money for a mere 1½ points. While there may be nothing wrong with this, let's not try to kid ourselves into thinking that we are getting into a hedged position. Sure, on the upside if everything works out right and the index is up 23 points at expiration you will make those 23 points plus your 1½ on the sale of the option. But note that almost the entire profit comes from the movement of the index, not from the sale of the option. On the other side, if the index goes down, those 1½ points you took in may give you protection for all of twenty minutes, or perhaps not even that long. In other words, you have no meaningful protection whatsoever, and even if the index does move in your direction, you are not adding any meaningful profit by the sale of the call. Thus it is not a true hedging position at all but merely an ornament, like a tattered old scarecrow in a cornfield. It may make the farmer feel better, but it certainly won't scare off the crows. So if you want to think that you have some downside protection, there is no way anyone can stop you, but please realize that you are only fooling yourself. Why not just go long a contract and recognize what you are doing?

4. *Take action when the index moves against you.* If the market has moved against you away from the option strike price and you are a covered option writer, you should carefully consider altering your position before expiration. The reason is that when the index moves away, the price of the option comes down and you have already realized most of the benefit from the option. From now on, if the index moves against you, you have virtually no protection, and furthermore, by now you have probably lost more money in the index than you could have made from the option. For example, if you took a long position in an index at 150 and sold the 150 option for 4, and the index has since declined to 140 and the option is now 1, you should consider your choices for taking action. You now have an unrealized loss of 10 points in your contract, and whereas you had 4 points of downside protection from the option when you started and also 4 points of possible profit from the option, you now have only 1 point. It really doesn't make sense to continue that position. One test is to ask yourself whether you would put on a new position like it. Would you want to buy the index at 140 and write the 150 option for 1? If not, then you should not want to stay in the position either. There are a number of possibilities.

• Close out both sides of the position. You might conclude that the index is likely to continue down and that since the 1 point left in the option clearly gives no meaningful downside protection, it's best to take your loss and get out of the position by buying in the option and selling out the long position in the index.

• Buy in the option and sell the next farther-out option—that is, roll out the option. Assume that you sold the March 150 and that with the passage of time there are now only a few weeks left in its life. With the March 150 at 1, the June 150 call might be at 4. If you still have faith that the index is not going to go down much farther, and indeed has a good possibility of coming back up, it makes sense to buy in the March call for 1 and sell the June for 4, giving you a net credit of 3 points on the trade. You have taken in an additional $1,500 on the trade, and once again you have 4 points of downside protection plus the opportunity to make those 4 points of profit from the expiration of the option.

• Buy in the option and sell the same expiration with a lower strike price, which is called rolling down the option. If we take the same facts as the last example, where your index has declined to 140 and the 150 option to 1, another possibility is to buy in the March 150 call and sell the March 140 call, which might very well be selling for 4 points. If you do this you are taking in an additional 3 points, which means that you have taken in a total of 7 points from the sale of options. The negative aspect is that by lowering the strike price by 10 points you have locked in a 10-point loss on the index. Once you do roll down to the 140 option there is no way you can make money on the position, and in fact you are doomed to lose at least 3 points. But this may be better than doing nothing, because you have taken in those additional 3 points, which will go toward reducing your loss if the index remains where it is or goes down farther.

• Buy in the option and sell the one of next farther-out duration with a lower strike price. This is known as rolling down and out. Using the same example, you would buy in the March 150 call and sell the June 140 call. The advantage over either of the other two previous possibilities is that you will be taking in significantly more money from the sale of this option. If the June 150 is 4 and the March 140 is also selling for 4, the June 140 might be selling for 10. Thus buying in the option and selling the June 140 would give you a credit of 9 points. When you add in the original 4 points you got from the March 150 call you have a total income from options of 13, which means that you could come out of this with a small profit. If the index remains at 140 or better upon the expiration of the June 140 call, you will have a loss of 10 points in the index and a profit of 13 from the options, giving you a profit of 3 points on the transaction. This is a reasonable profit when you consider that the index has actually declined and that you went into this position because you believed it would not.

The disadvantage of rolling down and out is that you are now committed to the position for an additional three months, and the total profit for a period of six months or so is quite limited. Furthermore, should the index come back up to 150, you will not be able to benefit from that move. Nevertheless, this technique is most frequently used when the index has moved down over a period of time.

When the index moves down suddenly in a short period of time, it is generally preferable simply to roll down without going out in time, because the lower strike-price options of the same expiration date will still have a fairly high price.

5. *Consider closing out the options before they expire.* There are two reasons why one writes options. The first is to make money from the expiration of the time value of the option, and the second is to get the downside protection in case the index moves against you. Neither one of these objectives can be fulfilled when the option has gone down to only a small fraction of its original value. In our example where you took a position in the index at 150 and sold the March 150 call for 4, assume that the index has remained at 150 but with the passage of time the option has declined to ½. You are still facing the same risk of the index falling, and if it does you have nothing between you and a loss except that tiny ½ point. Second, you are trying to make a profit from the option, and the only profit you can make is that minuscule ½ point. Therefore, from the point of view of both of your objectives it makes sense to buy in your option before it expires. Give up that extra ½ point by buying in the option and then doing something to take in a bigger premium. In the previous section we discussed doing this when the index has moved against you, and here we are suggesting that this be done even when the index is unchanged, or when you wrote an out-of-the-money option when the index has moved in your favor. If the index has remained at about the same level, you will probably simply write the next expiration option at the same strike price. But if the index has moved up, you might be able or want to write the option at the next higher strike price—that is, to "roll up." By not waiting for your option to expire but by buying it in when it has reached a small fraction of the original price, you will ensure that you always have a good potential profit ahead of you and that you have meaningful downside protection.

6. *Buy the index and write the option simultaneously.* You might assume if you are putting on a position which requires buying the index and selling the option that you would do the two at the same time, but of course there is no regulation which says it must be done that way. And in fact there is a great temptation to do it the other way. For

example, a person may say that he is going to try to put on his position on the index when it is down a bit, and then he will wait until it has gone up a few points to sell the option so he can get a much better price for it. What's wrong with that? After all, isn't it the American way to use a little ingenuity to get a better deal? Yes, if it works, but not if you merely are playing dangerous games. And unfortunately that is what happens here. The reason that putting on the index position first and then waiting for it to go up before selling the option is so dangerous is that it defeats the very reason for selling the option in the first place, which was to give yourself a partial hedge in case it goes down. So here is a person taking on all the risk of a long position on a stock index and deliberately saying that at first he is not going to be hedged, because he thinks the index will move up. If he were so sure the index is going to move up, then he wouldn't need to sell the option at all. Just close out the index after it has risen.

What would you think of a person who is buying a house and plans to get fire insurance on it but says he is going to save money by not getting the insurance until he has owned the house for a few months because he doesn't think there is any likelihood of the house burning down just after he has bought it? That is just about what would be happening here. Sure, the index might move up, and the person could sell the option at a higher price, just as he wanted to do. Great; he made a little extra money. But what if the index moves down? Then he is in the position of having lost money on the index with no offset from the sale of the option. And even worse is that if he decides to give up on the index ever going up and to sell the option at its present price, he will be receiving substantially less for it than he could have had in the beginning. In summary, if you want to be a covered writer, it should be because you believe in the concept of hedging your position, and if you believe in the concept, then you should believe in it at all times, not just when you don't need it.

7. *Before you put on the position, analyze the relationship of the return from the sale of the option to the risk you are taking and the potential profit you can make.* There are times when writing covered options make sense, and there are times when it does not. Since you are assuming the risk of taking a position in an index and are giving up some of the potential profit, carefully weigh the pros and cons before you decide whether it is worth doing. The key to your decision is the volatility of the index compared to the price of the option. Volatility simply means the probability that the index will move by a certain amount within a

certain period of time. The easiest way to ascertain this is by looking at a chart of the index and seeing over the past years just how much it has gone up or down in a typical three-month period. Then compare that to the amount you will be getting for the option. Generally the option premiums will be high when the recent history of the index has been volatile. For example, if the index has just gone up 20 points to a new all-time high, the premium of the option should be high. If the index has done nothing for a few months except meander a few points up and down, the options will be cheap. That of course is when you do not want to sell them.

STRATEGY RULES FOR UNCOVERED OPTION SELLERS

There are other specific rules of strategy for uncovered option writers.

1. *Selling a combination of a put and a call is recommended over selling just a put or a call.* There are two reasons for this recommendation. The first is that you are less likely to lose a lot of money on a combination. This can be illustrated by an example. Assume that the index is at 150 and you decide to write the 160 call for 4 and the 140 put for 3, taking in a total of 7 points. We hope that at no time prior to the options' expiration does the index go above 160 or below 140 and that both of the options expire for a profit to you of 7 points. But, out there in the harsh real world, events often don't go just quite as we would like. Let's say that the index takes off and gets up to 160, which you have decided is going to be your closing point. You buy in the call for 7 and show a loss of 3 points. But what about that 140 put which you sold for 3? With the index up 10 points, that has shrunken in value to just ½. Therefore you could buy it in for a profit of 2½, or you could wait until it expires and get the full profit of 3, assuming that the index does not reverse itself and fall back to 140. What either of these means is that your loss on the call of 3 points has been reduced to a mere ½ point or eliminated altogether. Thus you can convert a loss into a break-even situation in many circumstances and a much smaller loss in all cases if you write a combination instead of a put or a call alone.

The disadvantage of a combination is that the chance of losing on one of the two positions is just about twice as high as losing with a single option, but when you do lose, the loss will be so much less because the other option will be profitable. Since there is so much profit in uncovered call or put writing when it works out, but the loss can be so great when it does not, it makes good sense to write combinations to reduce the amount of loss when there is a loss.

The second reason for writing combinations is that the amount of profit can be so much greater. This is due to the method of computing the amount of margin required to write an uncovered position. When you sell an uncovered put and call, the margin department of your brokerage firm will figure out how much margin is required for each one and will then charge you with the margin only on the higher one. There is thus no margin requirement for the option which has the lesser requirement. In other words, you are selling one of them free. Therefore you naturally have the potential for making almost twice as much money from the same amount of capital when you sell a combination instead of only a put or only a call.

2. *Don't shy away from naked out-of-the-money puts or calls.* The beginner will often be attracted to the high prices of the on-the-money or close-to-the-money options without considering that he must provide a high amount of margin to write these options and that if the market moves against him he is in trouble much sooner than if he had written an out-of-the-money option. The way to determine how much money you can make from an uncovered option is not just to look at the price of the option but to determine how many dollars of option money you can take in with a given amount of margin money. To do this you have to figure out the margin requirement for each of the options, and you will often find that the farther-out-of-the-money options being in a greater amount of money per margin dollar than the higher-priced, near-to-the-money options. So they are actually making more money for you, and as we said, they will not get into trouble at the first slight move of the market against you. Furthermore, an out-of-the-money call-writing program can be thought of as a sort of hedge in conjunction with a stock portfolio, if you happen to own one. If the index goes up so much that you have to cover your out-of-the-money calls, then it is almost certain that you are making money on your stock portfolio, and a loss on your uncovered options will have been made up on the stocks.

3. *Be willing to redeploy your options constantly.* What is the best uncovered option position when you initially sell your options is probably not going to be the best six weeks later. And one of the advantages of naked option selling is that you have extreme flexibility. You are not anchored down to any index or any stock but free to rearrange your positions whenever you want. So if you have written

a December 170 call and the index has fallen by 10 points, you should probably roll down to the December 160 call. The chances are that you will have already made most of the possible profit from the 170 call you originally sold, so there is little point in hanging onto it just to make an additional fraction. Rather you can buy it in, and then sell the lower one with the possibility of picking up an additional profit.

The same thing can work in reverse. Let's say you sold the December 170 call when the market was 160 and now it has come up to 170, which you previously determined to be your stop-loss position. Therefore you buy in the 170 call. Now might be a very good time to write the 180 call instead of just getting out.

With combinations you can do the same thing with both parts of the combination. Let's say the market has gone up to the stop-loss point on your calls. You buy them in at a loss, and you rewrite the ones 10 points higher. At the same time, you could buy in your original puts at a good profit and sell the ones 10 points higher with the hope of making another profit. In other words, you are moving up both your puts and your calls by 10 points.

Also consider buying in your options even if nothing much has happened to the index, because your options will have shrunken over time. If you wrote a 150 call for 4, and now time has passed and it is worth only ½, remember that you are taking the same risk of loss as you were when it was 4, namely that the index will go above the strike price and you will have to buy in the option, but you aren't getting paid as much for taking the risk. So carefully consider buying in the option, then selling the next expiration period.

Appendixes

A. Specifications of Market Indexes
B. Glossary of Terms
C. Sources of More Information
D. The Eight Biggest Mistakes in Stock-Index Trading

APPENDIX A   SPECIFICATIONS OF INDEXES

	Value Line Composite Average	Standard & Poor's 500 Index
Underlying stocks	Approximately 1,700 stocks covered by **Value Line Investment Survey;** 90% traded on the NYSE; represents 96% of all dollar trading volume in U.S. equity markets	400 industrial, 40 utilities, 20 transportation and 40 financial companies; all on NYSE; represents 80% of value of all issues traded on NYSE
Method of computing average	Equal weight to all stocks; geometric average	Each stock weighted according to number of shares outstanding
Where traded	Kansas City Board of Trade	Index and Option Market Division of Chicago Mercantile Exchange
Options	No	Yes, on futures
Futures	Yes	Yes
Value of index	Times $500	Times $500
Expiration date of securities	Last trading day of contract month	Third Tuesday of contract month
Futures initial margin requirement	$6,500	$6,000
Options strike prices	5-point interval	5-point intervals
Ticker symbol of index	KVLI	INX
Ticker symbol of options		Calls: CS; puts: PS
Ticker symbol of futures	KV	SP

New York Stock Exchange Composite Index	CBOE-100 Index	Major Market Index
All common stocks listed on NYSE.	100 stocks on which options are traded on the Chicago Board Options Exchange; includes many major blue chips	20 major blue chip stocks
Each stock weighted according to number of shares outstanding	Each stock weighted according to number of shares outstanding	Equal weight to each stock, arithmetic average
New York Futures Exchange (a subsidiary of the New York Stock Exchange)	Chicago Board Options Exchange	American Stock Exchange
Yes, on futures	Yes	Yes
Yes	No	No
Times $500	Times $100	Times $100
Business day prior to last business day in the contract month	Business day prior to Saturday following third Friday of expiration month.	Saturday following third Friday of expiration month
$3,500	—	—
Even numbers (80, 82, 84, etc.)	5-point intervals	5-point intervals
NYQ	OEX	XMI
YX	OEX	XMI
YX	—	—

Standard Times for all securities: trading hours—10:00 A.M.—4:15 P.M. Eastern Time (until 4:00 P.M. on expiration date); expiration months: March, June, September, December, except Major Market Index options which are January, April, July and October.

Glossary of Terms

Asked. As used in the phrase "bid and asked," it is the price at which a potential seller is willing to sell; in other words, this is his asking price for what he is selling.

At the market. An order to buy or sell immediately at the best price available when the order is executed on the exchange.

Basis. The difference between the price of a cash commodity, here the price of the actual stock index, and the price of a specific futures contract for that index.

Bear. An investor who believes that stock prices will decline. His strategies are to buy puts, sell naked calls, and sell stock-index futures short.

Bear spread. A spread which makes money when stock prices go down. A bear spread consists of selling the option with the lower strike price and buying the option with the higher strike price. A bear spread with calls is a credit spread, a bear spread with puts is a debit spread.

Beta. A figure that indicates the historical propensity of a stock price to move with the stock market as a whole. The lowest theoretical Beta is 0, which indicates no movement, and the highest is 2, indicating wild gyrations for small movements in the market.

Bid. The price at which a potential buyer is willing to buy; he is bidding that amount to purchase the security offered. As used in "bid and asked prices," the two prices give the current market for an option or stock-index future.

Bull. An investor who believes that stock prices will rise. He buys calls, sells puts and goes long stock-index futures.

Bull spread. A spread which makes money when stock prices go up. It consists of buying the lower strike-price option and selling the higher strike-price option. A bull spread with calls results in a debit, and with puts in a credit.

Calendar spread. Buying a long-duration option or future and selling a shorter-duration option or future.

Call. An option giving the buyer the right to purchase an index or a future on an index for a given price within a given period of time.

Cash value. The value which an option has if it were to be exercised now. It is the amount by which an option is in the money. If an index is now 122, the 120 call has a cash value of 2 points. Also known as intrinsic value. Out-of-the-money options have no cash value. Compare FUTURE TIME VALUE.

CBOE. The Chicago Board Options Exchange, which opened April 26, 1973, as the first exchange in the world for stock options. Where options on the CBOE-100 are traded.

Cemetery spread. What happens to a spread when the index goes in the wrong direction. The spreader gets killed. An example of the humor(?) of Wall Street.

Closing price. The price at which transactions are made just before the closing bell. For options there is one closing price, but for futures there may be a range of prices. See also SETTLEMENT PRICE.

Closing transaction. The sale of an option or future by someone owning the option or long the future. Or the purchase of an option or future by a person who previously sold it short. These transactions terminate the investor's position.

Cover. To close out one's position. A trader who is short a December VLCA future may decide that he has made a mistake and that he had better get out of the position. He will cover his position by purchasing the future.

Covered call writer or seller. A call seller (writer) who is long a future on the calls he sells. By being long the index he is protected from any loss by an increase in the price of the index during the duration of the call.

Credit spread. A spread which produces money upon its execution—for example, selling a 35 call for 4 and buying a 40 call for 1. A credit spread has a margin requirement and makes money when the credit decreases.

Day orders. Orders which are valid only for the day entered.

Debit spread. A spread which produces a debit upon execution—for example, buying a December call for 4 and selling a September call for 1. A debit spread makes money when the amount of the spread decreases.

Deep in the money. An option which has a large cash or intrinsic value because the price of the index has moved far beyond the option strike price. A call is deep in the money when the index is much higher than the strike price, and a put is deep in the money when the index is far below the strike price.

Delivery. A term used in commodities to mean the tender and receipt of the cash commodity, or of documents covering such commodity, in settlement of a futures contract. Since stock indexes are abstract concepts which cannot be "delivered," the concept here simply means that the future is extinguished and replaced by the cash value of the actual index.

Delivery month. A commodity term used to designate the month in which the futures contract expires.

Diagonal spread. A spread in which a long-term option of one strike price is purchased and a shorter-term option of another strike price is sold. A common example is to purchase a long-term call at, say, a 40 strike price and sell the shorter-term 45 call. Basically a bullish spread.

Exercise. To do what an option gives one the right to do—for example, in the case of a call to purchase a future for the strike price or to acquire the cash value of an index for a cost equal to the strike price. In the case of a put it is the right to sell at a fixed price. Options need not be exercised, since they can always be sold for approximately the same profit that would be made by exercising them and immediately closing out the position.

Exercise price. The price at which the buyer of a call can purchase the underlying index during the life of the call, and the price at which the buyer of a put can sell the underlying future during the life of the put. Also called *strike price*.

Expiration date. The date on which the option or future becomes null and void—that is, the final date on which it may be exercised. See Appendix A for dates of different options and futures expirations.

Future time value. That part of the option price which does not represent cash value. Future time value is the excess which option buyers are willing to pay to obtain leverage and to limit exposure. It is the only part of the option price which produces a profit for the covered writer. In the case of out-of-the-money options, the entire option price is future time value.

Futures contract. A standardized contract for the purchase and sale of commodities for delivery during a specific month under set terms and conditions. With respect to stock indexes the delivery has been replaced by a substitution for the cash value of the underlying index.

GTC (good till canceled). An order to buy or sell that remains in effect until it is executed or is canceled by its originator.

Hedge. A transaction consisting of two or more separate transactions with the objective of providing a greater chance of making a profit, although perhaps a smaller one, than a single transaction.

In the money. An option worth money because of the current market price of the index. A call would be in the money if the current price of the index is above the strike price of the call.

Intrinsic value. See CASH VALUE.

Legging. As in legging in a position. Executing one side of a two- (or more) part position first, in the hope that the index will then move in the right direction so that the other side of the position can be executed at a more favorable price. One can also leg out of a position with the same objective. Opposite of executing something as a spread, which means doing both sides simultaneously.

Limit order. An order given to a broker which has some restrictions, such as price or time. For example, "Buy 2 March S&P 500 contracts at 148.75." The broker cannot pay more than that amount.

Liquid market. A market where selling and buying can easily be accomplished because there is a large number of buyers and sellers so that large quantities can be traded with small price differences.

Long. One who has bought futures or options. A person who is long a future will make money if the index rises in price.

Margin. The amount of money that must be deposited with a broker to buy or sell a security.

Market order. An order to buy or sell immediately at the best price available when the order enters the exchange.

Market, the. The market for a particular security consists of the current bid and offer prices on the floor of the exchange. This tells the potential customer the probable price if he wishes to buy or sell.

Mark to the market. The process of adjusting a margin account each day to the current prices of the underlying securities.

Naked-option writer or seller. One who sells (writes) a call without being long the underlying index in contrast to a covered call writer. The naked call writer may be able to make a higher return on his money, but he faces an unlimited liability if the index rises. Also, one who sells a put without being short the index.

Offer. An offer indicates a desire to sell at a given price. The offering price is always higher than the bid price, which is the price at which someone is willing to buy.

Open interest. The number of calls or futures outstanding at any time. Unlike shares of stock issued by corporations, usually via a formal registration statement, calls and futures are issued any time an investor decides to sell one. Thus the open interest fluctuates daily.

Open order. An order good until canceled.

Opening price. The first price of the day. In options this is a single price, but for futures it may be a range of prices recorded during the official opening period.

The New Stock Index Market

Option. A legal right allowing the owner to buy or sell an index or a futures contract on an index at a specific price during a specific period. A *call* is an option allowing its owner to buy at a specific price, and a *put* is an option allowing its owner to sell at a specific price.

Out of the money. An option that, because of the difference between the strike price and the market price of the underlying index, will be worth nothing unless the index moves in price. A call is out of the money when its strike price is above the current price of the index.

Parity. When the price of an option or future is equal to its cash value. Thus, if an index is 122, the 120 strike-price call is at parity if it is 2, and the future is at parity if it is 122.

Point. The minimum unit in which changes in an index may be expressed. The minimum move of stock-index futures is 5 points.

Position. To be either long or short in the market. One who buys a futures contract has a long position, while one who sells has a short position.

Premium. The price that the buyer pays the writer for an option (the term is synonymous with the price of an option).

Put. An option giving the owner the right to sell an index or a futures contract on an index for a specified price within a stated period of time. The purchaser of a put profits from a decline in the price of the index.

Settlement price. A discrete price, set by futures market officials under established rules, which is based upon that day's closing price range. It is the price used as the official closing price for determining daily gains and losses and margin requirements.

Short. To be short a security means to owe it to someone. Whereas the investor who is long buys a security and then sells it, hopefully for a higher price, the short seller sells the security first, then buys it back later, hopefully for a lower price.

Spreading. The purchase of one security against the sale of another security, both of which are based upon the same underlying stock index. A spread is made with the expectation that the price relationships between the two securities will change, so that a subsequent closing transaction will yield a profit.

Stop-loss order. An order entered with a specific price. The current market, however, is better than the price in the order, and the order is only to be filled when the market goes against the person entering the order. For example, if a futures contract is now at 110, a stop-loss order might be entered to buy the contract at 112. It is the opposite of a limit order, whose purpose is to execute an order at a better price than the current market.

Straddle. A position consisting of a put and a call on the same index for the same strike price. Each option may be exercised separately. It makes money if the index moves either up or down far enough.

Strike (or striking) price. The price at which the buyer of a call can purchase the index or future during the life of the option, and the price at which the buyer of a put can sell them during the life of the option. Also called EXERCISE PRICE.

Time spread. See CALENDAR SPREAD.

Uncovered. See NAKED-OPTION WRITER OR SELLER.

Vertical spread. Buying one option and selling an option on the same index with a different strike price, usually with the same duration. Bull spreads and bear spreads are examples.

Writer. The grantor of an option contract. Also called the *maker* or the *seller*. Further divided into COVERED WRITERS, who own the underlying index, and NAKED WRITERS, who do not.

Appendix C

The first place to request information is from your own broker, who should be able to supply you with booklets describing the indexes, options and futures. To obtain more information on stock indexes, contact the exchanges on which the futures or options are traded. Each of the exchanges has done an excellent job of producing booklets which explain the various aspects of their products in clear and concise language. Here is a list of some of the literature available from the exchanges:

KANSAS CITY BOARD OF TRADE

As you may recall, this exchange started it all. They have a brief introductory booklet titled *The Future Is Here: Value Line Average Stock Index Futures*. In addition, they have a series of larger booklets each with the general title *The Future Is Here* and a specific subtitle. The various subtitles are: *Value Line Composite Average: The Index Behind the Futures; Futures Trading & The Value Line Stock Index; Hedging & Speculating in Value Line Futures;* and *Option Strategies & Stock Index Futures*.

Each of these booklets is available free of charge from:
Kansas City Board of Trade
Marketing Department
4800 Main St., Suite 274
Kansas City, Mo. 64112
Tel.: (816) 753-7500

INDEX AND OPTION MARKET DIVISION OF CHICAGO MERCANTILE EXCHANGE
(Standard & Poor's 500)

Perhaps the best publications of any exchange have been produced by the Chicago Merc. Their introductory booklet on S&P 500 futures is called *Opportunities in Stock Futures*. A more detailed booklet designed primarily for institutional investors is called *Inside S&P 500 Stock Index Futures*, which contains a great deal of useful theoretical material.

The basic introduction booklet on options is titled *Options on Futures: A New Way to Participate in Futures*; and a more detailed booklet is called *Inside S&P 500 Options: The Ultimate Option*. In addition to these booklets, they have prepared films explaining option and futures; these films can be rented by brokers and others planning meetings on the S&P 500. To obtain this information contact:

168

Index and Option Market
c/o Chicago Mercantile Exchange
444 W. Jackson Blvd.
Chicago, Ill. 60606
Tel.: (312) 648-1000
or 67 Wall St.
New York, N.Y. 10005
Tel.: (212) 363-7000
or 27 Throgmorton
London EC2N 2AN
England
Tel.: 011/441/920-0722

NEW YORK FUTURES EXCHANGE (NYFE)

The NYFE puts out a small booklet called *New York Stock Exchange Composite Index Futures Contract Specifications*, and their major publication on futures is titled *Introducing New York Stock Exchange Index Futures*. They have an excellent booklet on options called *The Option for the Future*. These may be obtained from:

New York Futures Exchange
20 Broad St.
New York, N.Y. 10005
Tel.: (212) 623-4949

CHICAGO BOARD OPTIONS EXCHANGE (CBOE-100)

The basic introductory booklet of the CBOE is called *The CBOE 100 Index: The Option Edge*. Undoubtedly as time goes by they will issue more publications dealing with different aspects of their options. For further information contact:

The Chicago Board Options Exchange
LaSalle at Jackson
Chicago, Ill. 60604

BOOKS

A great many books have been published on commodities futures. A very informative one is *The Commodity Futures Game* by Richard J. Teweles, Charles V. Harlow and Herbert L. Stone. The book is well written and contains a great deal of serious information on the practice and theory of futures. One chapter, called "The Commodity School for Losers," is a spoof on the different types of traders who have a system which "can't lose"; this chapter is so funny that it alone is worth the price of the book, published in 1977 and available in paperback in an abridged edition (359 pages) for $5.95. It is published by McGraw-Hill Book Company, 1221 Avenue of the Americas, New York, N.Y. 10020.

For a book which can provide more detailed knowledge on options, we modestly suggest the best-selling book in the field of stock options. Although the subject is not identical, there is enough in this book on the theory of options which does apply to options on indexes to make it worthwhile for someone seeking a more detailed discussion. The book, published in 1979, is by Max G. Ansbacher and is the revised edition of *The New Options Market*. It costs $16.95 and is published by Walker & Company, 720 Fifth Avenue, New York, N.Y. 10019.

Appendix D

The Eight Biggest Mistakes in Stock Index Trading

When things go wrong we tend to blame unfortunate circumstances which we believe are beyond our control. And yet, in the stock-index market as in life, these "uncontrollable" circumstances can be prevented, if we take care to avoid these basic mistakes:

1. Having all one's stop-loss orders at the same price. If you are long five contracts at 165, you may conclude that if the price ever gets down to 161, that is the time to get out of the market. So you place a stop-loss order at 161 for all your contracts. It is very possible that the price can suddenly go right down to 161 setting off your orders, and then head straight back up all the way to 165. You'll be feeling pretty bad. This is such a pathetic mistake because the solution is so simple: Just stagger your stop-loss orders at various prices, such as one at each of the following points: 161.80, 161.40, 161.00, 160.60 and 160.20. Then, even if the contract does go down to 161, at least you have gotten out of some of your positions at higher prices, and you will still have two of your contracts in case it goes back up in price. If it keeps going down, the average price you receive for all your contracts will be the same 161.

2. Thinking that stock indexes are an easy way to get rich. This is an easy error to understand. For example, you may take a position in a future with an initial cash requirement of $6,000. In the first day the future is up 1 point, and the next day it is up 2 points, for a profit of $1,500. In just two days you're ahead by 25%. Wow! That's fantastic. But of course, you know that you were lucky to be able to make 25% in just two days. In the future it might take a week to make that much. That would be a profit of 100% a month, without compounding. Not bad. At the end of a year you would be up by 1,200%, and again to be conservative we will ignore compounding. That means if you start with $10,000, you will end up with $130,000. Pretty good. But the real fun starts in the second year. Undoubtedly you will be getting better at this as you go along, but assuming that you just use the same conservative figures as you did in the first year, you would end up the second year with $1,690,000.

The only trouble with this is that it is just plain absurd. One week of losses will totally change everything. And you *will* have losses, sooner or later. So don't despair when the losses occur, and don't think that you can extrapolate a few lucky trades into a year's results.

3. Switching from long to short or vice versa every time you lose money. Some speculators are so flighty that when they see that they are losing in a long position, they immediately conclude that the market is going to hell, and they rush in to go short. Then if the market starts going up, they decide that they were wrong once again, and they quickly go long to catch this new trend up. This kind of trading, if done for short intra day moves, means that you pay a lot in commissions, but more importantly it gives you the opportunity to be wrong almost all the time. If a market has just gone down, there is more of a chance over the short term that it will come back up, and of course the corollary is just as true.

One study of various stock-index-futures trading patterns found that of all those studied, this one was the worst. It does give you the sense that you are doing a lot, but unfortunately it is all too often a lot of just exactly the wrong thing. Far better to take a position and stick with it to a predetermined level and then get out of the market for a while and consider your next move, rather than calling yourself a dunce and running in the opposite direction.

4. Buying stock-index options too far out-of-the-money. We start with the proposition that purchasing stock-index options is a very speculative endeavor. But even in this risky world, there are different degrees of risk. It is my contention here that even normal, on-the-money or just out-of-the-money options are risky. To make money with an on-the-money option, say with a 160 strike-price option when the index is at 160, the index has to move up by more than the cost of the option. But if you buy an out-of-the-money option like the 170, the index has to move up 10 points plus the cost of the option before you can make any money at the expiration date.

This makes it so unlikely that you will win, that buying one of these options becomes something like buying a lottery ticket. And I don't buy lottery tickets with my money.

5. Not using stop-loss orders to limit losses in futures. The possible swings in an index future are enormous and almost everyone recognizes that simply to stay with a future while it is going against you can lead to virtual financial ruin. Yet many traders do not use stop-loss orders because they always seem to get you out at the wrong time, selling at the low of the day and buying in at the high.

These traders say it is better to talk with your broker frequently and then use your judgment on when to get out. This argument sounds fine, but it doesn't work out very well in practice. Suppose you are long some contracts, and your broker tells you that they're down 1.50 on the day. Now what do you do? What divine inspiration tells you that this is the low for the day and you should do nothing, or that this is the beginning of a major bear market and you should get out immediately? Since there is nothing which can give you that answer, you might just as well use a stop-loss order. And the big advantage of a stop-loss order is that it does not wonder if this is or is not the worst time to sell. This wondering has cost traders millions of dollars over the years. Stop-loss orders don't think, because you have done the thinking in advance for them. They simply carry out your orders like good soldiers.

6. Relying completely upon "technical" factors. By "technical" factors, I am referring here to chart reading, or to relying upon how the Dow Jones Industrial Average moves. If the average goes above a certain designated number, such as 1200, it indicates to the technical analyst that the market has broken out and will continue to zoom. If the average goes below another designated number, it indicates that a resistance point has been broken and that the market will continue to go straight down. It has been my experience that most "technical" analysts are right about half the time, and for our purposes this is simply not good enough.

Therefore, when trading stock-index futures, and to a lesser extent options, you must place just as much emphasis on your trading strategies, i.e., stop-loss levels and limit-order levels, as you do on your favorite guru's predictions of things to come.

7. Not using potentially profitable techniques because of the fear of unlimited losses. There is no question that trading stock-index futures, and selling uncovered stock-index options, can lead to enormous losses, and that the great majority of investors are not suited for these techniques because they do not have sufficient net worth and liquid assets to permit them to risk the large losses that these methods can bring. But, it is precisely because so many individuals and institutions are prohibited from entering the arena that, in my opinion, larger than normal returns can be made here. For example, if everyone wants to buy stock-index options, but few people are willing to sell them, aren't the prices going to be very favorable to the sellers?

The profit potential in trading stock-index future contracts is shown in the following example. This account started in March 1982 under my management with $100,000 and realized profits of $18,756 through December 1982. Then in January 1983 it realized profits of $54,327; in February $34,161; in March $20,618; and in April $71,276. Clearly this is an exceptional performance and is not mentioned here to suggest that it will continue or that it is at all typical, but rather simply to show that the potential for high profit does exist. To forego this profit potential because of an unrealistic fear of the remote possibility of losing all one's money plus more, would be a great mistake for those who qualify.

8. Not having a plan. By this I mean a *written* plan detailing exactly what you will do when your index goes against you, and exactly what you will do when it goes in your favor. This topic was covered extensively in Chapter 3 and is repeated here for emphasis.

Trading stock indexes is hard work, and part of that work is thinking out a plan. The fact of the matter is that everyone has a plan. Some are as detailed and carefully constructed as the two in this book. Others are simply in the mind of the trader. And usually the unwritten plan is to play one's hunches. "G.M. had higher earnings? Buy!" "M-1 is up? Sell!" "New trouble in the Middle East? Buy gold, short the market!" These kind of knee-jerk reactions may make great Alka-Seltzer commercials, but they don't do much for your bottom line over any period of time. It is the person without any plan who gets pulled into buying at the highs and selling out at the lows in abject panic. Because he has nothing to sustain his judgment, no guiding light. It's your choice. Either you have a plan, or the market will create a plan for you. And the market is not looking out for your welfare.

INDEX

Aerospace subindexes, 11
Air transport subindexes, 11, 12
American Express, 11
American Stock Exchange
 index of, *see* Major Market Index
 number of stocks listed on, 6
 subindexes of, 12
 in VCLA, 9
Arbitrage in stock-index futures, 43–45
Arnold Bernhard Co., 9
Asked, definition of, 162
At the market, definition of, 162
AT&T, 10
Atlantic-Richfield, 11
Averaging up or down, 77–78

Basis, definition of, 162
Bear, definition of, 162
Bear spread, definition of, 162
Bell-curve effect, 137, 138
Betas
 definition of, 162
 in spreading strategies, 98–100
Bid, definition of, 162
Boeing, 11
Boise Cascade, 11
Books on commodity futures, 169–170
Bristol-Myers, 11
Brokers, *see* Dealers
Brown, Harry, 43
Bull, definition of, 162
Bull spread, definition of, 162
Buy-and-hold plan, 60–62, 77

Calendar spread (time spread),
 definition of, 162

Calls
    covered, 130–35, 142–43, 150–52,
        163
    definition of, 102–3, 162
    prices of, 104–8
        large differences for different
            months, 113
        puts compared, 113–114
    uncovered (naked), 135–39, 140–42,
        144–45, 165
Cash value (intrinsic value), definition
        of, 162
CBOE-100 Index, 163, 169
    description of, 10, 14, 161
    options on, 103–4
Cemetery spread, definition of, 163
Champion International, 11
Chicago Board Options Exchange
    index of, see CBOE-100 Index
    subindexes of, 11–12
Chicago Mercantile Exchange, S&P
    500 traded on, 8, 47, 168–69
Closing price
    definition of, 163
    See also Settlement price
Closing transactions, definition of,
        163
Coca-Cola, 11
Combination put and call, selling of,
        156–57
Commodity Exchange, Inc., 5
Commodities futures, traditional, 20–22
Computer subindex, 11
Cover, definition of, 163
Covered calls, 130–35, 142–43, 150–52,
        163
Credit limits for commodities account,
        54–55
Credit spread, definition of, 163

Day orders, definition of, 163
Day trades, commissions on, 45–46
Dealers (brokers)
    commissions not paid by, 44–45
    commissions to
        on stock-index futures, 45–47
        on stock-index options, 47
    suitability standards of, 54–55
Debit spread, definition of, 163

176

Deep-in-the-money options, 121–22
  covered call writing with, 132
  definition of, 163
Delivery
  definition of, 163
  of stock futures, 24–25
Delivery month, definition of, 163
Delta Air Lines, 11
Diagonal spread, definition of, 164
DJIA, *see* Dow Jones Industrial Average
Dow Chemical, 11
Dow Jones Industrial Average (DJIA)
  compared to other indexes, 12, 61
  description of, 6–7
  over-reliance on, 172–73
Drug subindexes, 11, 12

Eastman Kodak, 10
Electronic Instrumentation and
      Components Index, 12
Exercise, definition of, 164
Exercise price, *see* Strike price
Expectations of investors, 39–40
Expiration dates
  definition of, 164
  of stock-index futures, 16, 32, 37–39
  of stock-index options, 103, 122–24
Exxon, 10, 11

Federal Express, 11
Financial Services Index, 12
Future time value, definition of, 164
Futures on stock indexes
  basic information on trading in, 16–18
  concept of, 23–24
  date of first trading in, 1
  delivery of, 24–25
  example of profit on, 1
  financial requirements for, 54–55
  margin for, *see* Margin—for stock-index
      futures
  newspaper reports on, 47–53
  opening accounts for, 53–54
  options compared to, 101–3, 108–14,
      118–19
  orders on, 32–36
  prices of, *see* Prices—of stock-index
      futures
  standardized contracts for, 164

terminating positions in, 31–32
trading strategies for, 56–100
  averaging up or down, 77–78
  buy and hold, 60–62, 77
  flexibility, 85
  hedging, 95–97
  need to limit losses, 62–71
  need to take profits, 85–87
  number of contracts, 76
  short-term moves, 78–79
  for short-term trader, 89–93
  spreads, 97–100
  sticking with your plan, 88–89
  taking the initial position, 71–75
  for trader expecting major move,
    90, 93–94
  when you are making money, 79–85

General Dynamics, 11
General Electric, 10, 11
General Motors, 10, 11, 23
Gold futures, story about, 79–80
Good-faith deposit on stock-index
    futures, 53
Good-till-canceled (GTC) orders
  by covered option sellers, 146
  definition of, 164
  on stock-index futures, 36, 63–64, 76–77
Group indexes, *see* Subindexes
GTC orders, *see* Good-till-canceled
    orders

Hamilton, Mary T., 14
Harlow, Charles V., 169
Hedges
  definition of, 164
  stock-index futures as, 95–97
Holding and hoping, 83–84
Honeywell, 11
Hospital Management and Supplies Index,
    12

IBM, 10, 11
In-the-money options, 114–15, 117
  covered call writing with, 134–35
  definition of, 164
  uncovered call writing with, 137–39
  uncovered put writing with, 140
Indexes, *see* Stock indexes
Inflation, taking account of, 60

Informational Technology Index, 12
International Paper, 11
Intrinsic value (cash value), definition
    of, 162

Kansas City Board of Trade, 9, 168
  See also Value Line Composite Average
Kauffman, Henry, 86
Kennedy, John F., 69
Kodak, 11

Legging, definition of, 164–65
Leverage of call options compared to
    stock-index futures, 109, 118
Lifetime High or Low (in newspapers),
    48, 50
Limit orders
  definition of, 165
  on stock-index futures, 33–35, 83–84, 85
Liquid market, definition of, 165
Locked-in risk, 29
Long, definition of, 165
Lorie, James A., 14

Major Market Index
  compared to other indexes, 14, 15
description of, 11, 161
  options on, 103
Margin
  definition of, 165
  on options, 109
    on options on indexes, 143–44
    for selling uncovered options on
      futures, 140–42
  on stock-index futures, 18–20, 25–31,
    47
    calls, 27–28, 29–31
    losing more than your margin, 28–29
    Use of Treasury bills, 26, 28
Market, the, definition of, 165
Market orders
  definition of, 165
  on stock-index futures, 32–33
Marking to the market, 19
  definition of, 165
Maturities, *see* Expiration dates
Media/Entertainment Index, 12
Merchandising Index, 12
Mobil, 11
Morgan, J. P., 76

Naked calls, *see* Uncovered calls
NCR, 11
New York Futures Exchange (NYFE), 169
    Financial Index of, 11
New York Stock Exchange (NYSE) Index
    compared to other indexes, 12–15
    description of, 8–9, 161
    margin for
        current amount, 18, 26
        maintenance level, 27
    newspaper reporting of, 48
    options on, 103
Newspapers, futures prices in, 47–53
Northwest Air, 11
NYFE, *see* New York Futures Exchange
NYSE, *see* New York Stock Exchange
        Index

Offer, definition of, 165
Oil and gas (petroleum) indexes, 11,
        12
On-the-money options, 115, 117
    covered call writing with, 130–32
    uncovered put writing with, 139–40
Open interest
    definition of, 165
    in newspaper reports, 48, 50–51
Open orders, definition of, 165
Opening price
    definition of, 165
    in newspapers, 48, 49
Options on stock indexes, 101–58
    date of first trading on, 1
    definition of, 166
    expiration dates of, 103, 122–24
    margin on, *see* Margin—on options
    options on stock-index futures
        compared to, 103–4, 129
    prices of, *see* Prices—of options
    profit-taking from, 125–26
    rules of strategy for, 119–27
        for sellers, 145–58
    selling of, 128–58
        covered, 130–35, 142–43, 150–52,
            156–58, 163
        uncovered (naked), 135–39, 140–42,
            144–45, 156–58, 165
    stock-index futures compared to,
        101–3, 108–14, 118–19
    two basic types of, 103–4

See also Deep-in-the-money options;
    In-the-money options; On-the-money
    options; Out-of-the-money options;
    Puts
Orders, types of, on stock-index
    futures, 33–36
    See also Stop-loss orders
Out-of-the-money options, 115–118
    covered call writing with, 132–34,
        150–52
    definition of, 166
    risky nature of, 110–11, 119–21,
        172
    uncovered call writing with, 137,
        157
    uncovered put writing with, 140, 157
Owens-Illinois, 11

Paper and Forest Products Group, 11
Parity, definition of, 166
Petroleum (oil and gas) indexes, 11, 12
Point, definition of, 166
Position, definition of, 166
Planning, 56–59, 173–74
Premiums
    definition of 166
    on stock-index futures
        fluctuations of, 41–43
        option premiums compared to, 111–13
Prices
    of options, 104–108, 113
        annualization, 124–25
        calls compared to puts, 113–114
        large differences for different
            months, 113
        typical price decline (chart), 148
        volatility, 106–8
    of stock-index futures, 38–43, 113
        compared to indexes, 40–42
        effect of lost interest, 38–39
        market expectations, 39–40
        in newspapers, 47–53
        what price to enter market, 74
Puts, 105–6
    definitions of, 166
    prices of, compared to calls, 113–14
    risky nature of, 111
    selling of, 129–30
        uncovered, 139–40, 156–57
    See also Options on stock indexes

Pyramiding, 80–82

Raytheon, 11
Rockwell International, 11
Rogers, Will, 56
Rolling down and out, 153–54
Rolling over, 113

S&P 500, *see* Standard & Poor's
     500 Index
Salomon Brothers, 86
Settlement price
  definition of, 166
  in newspapers, 48–50
Short, definition of, 166
Southwest Air, 11
Sperry, 11
Spread, the, trading against, 72–74
Spreading
  definition of, 166
  definitions of various types of,
     162–64
  as stock-index futures strategy, 97–100
Squibb, 11
Staggered stop-loss orders, 67–68
Standard & Poor's 500 Index
  compared to other indexes, 12–14, 61
  description of, 7–8, 160
  example of profit on, 1
  information sources on, 168–69
  margin for
    current amount, 18, 26
    maintenance level, 27
  newspaper reporting of, 47–53
  options on, 103
Standard Oil (Indiana), 11
Stock indexes
  advantages of trading in, 2–4
  general description of, 5–6
  list of, 8–12
  relationship to each other, 12–13
  spreading of, 98–99
  See also Futures on stock indexes;
     Options on stock indexes;
     Subindexes
Stock portfolios, hedging of, 95–97
Stone, Herbert L., 169
Stop-limit orders on stock-index
     futures, 65

Stop-loss orders, 171
    definition of, 166–67
    by option sellers, 146–47
    on stock-index futures, 35–36, 63–71,
        76–77, 172
        being whipsawed, 65–67
        entry into market by, 74–75
        increasing of, when your are making
            money, 84–85
        keeping close to market price,
            68–69
        staggered stops, 67–68
Straddles, definition of, 167
Strike price (striking price; exercise
    price), 102–3, 107, 114
    definition of, 164, 167
Subindexes (group indexes)
    advantages of trading in, 3
    description of, 11–12
    in spreading strategies, 97–100
Suitability standards for commodities
        accounts, 54–55
Superior Oil, 11
Syntex, 11

Technical factors, over-reliance on,
        172–73
Teweles, Richard J., 169
Time spread (calendar spread),
        definition of, 162
Treasury bills for stock-index futures,
        26, 28

UAL, 11
Uncovered calls (naked calls), 135–39,
    140–42, 144–45, 165
    special rules of strategy for, 156–58
United Technologies, 11
Upjohn, 11

Value Line Composite Average (VCLA)
    booklets on, 168
    compared to other indexes, 12–15, 61
    description of, 9–10, 160
    margin for
        current amount, 18, 26
        maintenance level, 27
    newspaper reporting of, 48
    options on, 103
    price of stock-index futures compared
        to, 40–41

Wall Street Journal, futures prices in,
47–53
Weyerhaeuser, 11
Wheat futures, 20–22
Whipsawing, 65–67
Wishful-thinking syndrome, 83